T0195843

Strong Faith

WHAT WE AS WOMEN LEARN FROM SAMSON

7 WEEK BIBLE STUDY

DIANA S. PEREZ

WESTBOW
PRESS®
A DIVISION OF THOMAS NELSON
& ZONDERVAN

WestBow Press books may be ordered through booksellers or by contacting:

WestBow Press
A Division of Thomas Nelson & Zondervan
1663 Liberty Drive
Bloomington, IN 47403
www.westbowpress.com
844-714-3454

Because of the dynamic nature of the Internet, any web addresses or links contained in this book may have changed since publication and may no longer be valid. The views expressed in this work are solely those of the author and do not necessarily reflect the views of the publisher, and the publisher hereby disclaims any responsibility for them.

Any people depicted in stock imagery provided by Getty Images are models, and such images are being used for illustrative purposes only. Certain stock imagery © Getty Images.

Scripture quotations are taken from the New King James Version. Copyright © 1982 by Thomas Nelson, Inc. Used by permission. All rights reserved.

ISBN: 978-1-6642-9792-0 (sc)
ISBN: 978-1-6642-9791-3 (e)

Library of Congress Control Number: 2023907289

Print information available on the last page.

WestBow Press rev. date: 06/02/2023

INTRODUCTION

I chose Samson, because, even though he is a male figure from the Bible, there are many lessons we as women can learn from his life and apply to our lives today.

This women's Bible study is organized into seven weeks of group study and begins with a section called *Let's Dig In,* where we dig into God's Word and learn about Samson. Discussion questions are contained throughout.

Following each weekly study group session are five days of individual reflection time. Each one contains a section called *Let's Relate,* which has humorous personal stories I share, so you can get to know a little bit about me. The last section is called *Let's Explore,* which has a couple of questions to allow you to reflect and apply them to your personal life. Each day concludes with a short prayer.

I pray this study blesses you.

Diana

To Learn more about Diana, please visit www.handbagofhope.com
IG: @handbagofhope

WEEK 1

GOD'S DIVINE MESSAGES

DISCUSS: What do you hope to learn from this study?

Who was Samson?

Read Judges 2:18
And when the Lord raised up judges for them, the Lord was with the judge and delivered them out of the hand of their enemies all the days of the judge; for the Lord was moved to pity by their groaning because of those who oppressed them and harassed them.

Samson was a judge in the Bible who is said to have had more opportunities than other men of that day. A judge was the name primarily given to the military leaders or rulers who oversaw the affairs of the Israelites during the time between the death of Joshua, and before the monarchy was established and King Saul came on the scene. Joshua was appointed as successor after the death of Moses. The time of the judges was generally a time of confusion and anarchy because there was no king in Israel. Because of this lack of authority, this period was a time where everyone did what was right in their own eyes. Samson had a bright future ahead of him, but he struggled in many ways to receive and live God's calling on his life.

Why Samson?

You are probably wondering why we are at a women's Bible study and learning about Samson, one of the male characters from the Bible. Is it because he was a handsome mystery man from biblical times, with long hair and amazing muscles and strength? I always imagine a man like Fabio or Thor, who drew attention everywhere they went with their good looks and muscular physique.

DISCUSS: When you think of Samson, what type of man do you imagine?

What's interesting is that scripture tells us Samson moved through the cities unknown, which tells us he didn't physically stand out in stature or have lots of big muscles like the Hulk. Another indicator of his most likely average size is that the enemy couldn't figure out where his strength came from—another clue that it was not visible from the outside.

DISCUSS: Does the fact that Samson looked like an ordinary man surprise you?

God has a plan for all of us, and it does not matter our background, abilities, looks, intellect, or status. Many times, God uses the plain and weak things of this world to accomplish His purposes, so that others can see that He is our strength and that through Him we can do all things, as it is written in Philippians 4:13. Actually, there are quite a few lessons we women can learn not only from Samson, but from the women surrounding him, such as his mother, wife, Delilah, plus a prostitute from the city of Gaza. Our study starts with Samson's birth through his life story until the time of his death. We will learn how his story intertwines concepts such as lust, obedience, gratefulness, pride, self-sufficiency, obsession, and God's plan for our lives. By studying Samson's choices and patterns in life, we can learn about him, the women surrounding him, and how we can apply that knowledge to our lives today. God has a perfect plan for every one of us.

Let's Dig In…

Read Judges 13:1
Again the children of Israel did evil in the sight of the Lord, and the Lord delivered them into the hand of the Philistines for forty years.

Following God and then forgetting about Him and going their own way was a common theme with the Israelites. Notice that the scripture starts with the word "again." The account of Samson takes place during forty years of Israelite oppression imposed upon them by the Philistines, who were their worst enemies. The Philistines were strong and had many weapons that the Israelites had never even seen. They were also proficient in making iron and used this knowledge to intimidate the Israelites.

Our biblical account takes place in Zorah, which is a city several miles west of Jerusalem, and begins with a special message from an angel delivered to Samson's mother. We will refer to her as *Manoah's wife,* because her name is not provided in scripture. She was barren, unable to have children. The angel of the Lord told her that she would give birth to a son, and he would be a Nazarite, which was someone dedicated to God. His purpose was determined before he was born, and God marked him for a special assignment—Samson was to bring glory and honor to the Lord and to deter Philistine invasions.

DISCUSS: Where do we hear a similar message from an angel later in scripture?

Many chapters in the Old Testament start with the phrase, "Again, the children of Israel did evil in the sight of the Lord." Israel had entered another phase of idolatrous worship when the story of Samson began. The Lord used the Philistines to chasten or discipline Israel. Unlike other accounts in the Bible of Israel's disobedience, there is no record of Israel being repentant prior to God raising up Samson as a deliverer. The Israelites were in great distress because of their disobedience, and God allowed them to fall into the hands of their neighbors and enemies—the Philistines. This difficulty lasted forty years, which must have felt like an eternity. But then they called to God, and He heard them and raised up Samson.

God still hears us when we call to Him. He does not always answer in the way we would like, but He hears us and cares for us as His children. Don't underestimate your place as a woman. The Bible contains several accounts where God bypassed husbands and male guardians and spoke critically important messages directly to women. Where God did not speak personally, He sent angels or prophets. Each woman had a choice to make: were they going to be obedient to the Lord and His plan for their life or go their own way?

Much of the Old Testament is foreshadowing the coming of Christ in the New Testament. Samson's birth was miraculously similar to Christ's birth.

- Both births were foretold by an angel of the Lord.
- The angel appeared to the women (Manoah's wife and Mary) before appearing to their husbands.
- Both Samson and Jesus were set apart for God from the womb.
- Both were judges. Samson was the last of the judges of the ancient Israelites. Jesus was the coming judge who would judge both the living and the dead.
- Both moved in the power of the Spirit.
- Both were rejected by their own people.
- Both destroyed their enemies. Samson's enemy was the Philistines, and Christ's enemy was sin, death, and Satan.

Differences between both: Jesus' life was sinless. Samson lived a life of sin. In Luke 23:34, while on the cross, Jesus said to God, "Father, forgive them, for they know not what they do." Samson asked God if he could destroy his enemies for revenge. In death, Samson's arms were outstretched on the two pillars in vengeance on his enemies. Jesus' arms were outstretched on the cross in mercy, forgiveness, and love. Samson died, and Jesus rose again and lives in us if we accept Him.

Diana S. Perez

In this study, we will learn about God's plan for Samson's life and how that relates to God's plan for our lives. God always has a plan, and, even if we were a surprise to our mother and father, we were not a surprise to God. Nothing is an accident, and everything is according to God's magnificent and perfect plan. We were made by God and for God, and nothing will ever make sense until we comprehend that fact.

Read Psalms 139:14; 16
I will praise You, for I am fearfully and wonderfully made; Marvelous are Your works, And that my soul knows very well. Your eyes saw my substance, being yet unformed. And in Your book they were all written, The days fashioned for me, When as yet there were none of them.

DISCUSS: What does this verse in Psalms mean to you? Were you or anyone you know ever told your birth was an accident? Do you see God's truth that you were not a surprise to God, but that He has a specific plan for you?

PRAYER REQUESTS AND PRAYER

Individual Reflection Time - Week 1

Day 1

Let's Relate…

Early one morning I woke from a strange dream in which I was in a wheelchair being escorted through a crowded hallway for medical tests. Apparently, I was in labor. I looked disheveled and delirious, probably preparing me for what I would look like every day thereafter as a new mom.

I glanced down and saw a white metal band on my arm. It had five symbols, and it seemed to be sewn into my skin. I asked the nurse the meaning of the five symbols, and she said, "Horrendous, absolutely horrendous!" My hands went over my ears, and I refused to listen to her reply. That's when I suddenly awoke from my dream. Those must be the most accurate words my subconscious used to describe what would soon be my labor and delivery experience.

Let's Explore…

1. **Explain how you might have handled receiving an unexpected yet specific message like the one that Manoah's wife received?**

   _____

2. **What would have been the first thing you would have done after receiving the message?**

   _____

Read Romans 4:20-22
Dear Lord, help me to trust You when You are moving and working on my behalf. You are a good God and Your promises are always good. My assignment is to not waiver when I receive those promises or read about them in Your Word. I believe and need to hold fast until they manifest. Thank you that You give me the strength to stand firm and strong in You! Amen.

Day 2

Let's Relate...

Let me start at the beginning. Being 5'3" (really 5'2", but I like to round up, except for my weight—then I round down), I was in for a challenge when I became pregnant. I felt like my bottom was falling out and had every ache, pain, and 'oid in the book. Obviously, I was not a good pregnant woman. I couldn't wait for labor. Little did I know that I wouldn't be a good labor woman, either!

During my 40th week of pregnancy, my family and I attended a graduation ceremony at a large convention center. My father and I got locked in the stairwell while he was trying to help me locate a restroom. Had I listened to the attendant who told us not to go that way, we wouldn't have been in that predicament. There was no place to go but down. Having gained a whopping amount of weight, I considered four flights of stairs overwhelming. The challenging part was to step down each step when I couldn't see (or even imagine) where my feet were!

Let's Explore...

Take a few minutes and list areas where you believe God has gifted you. Remember that your gifts–your time, talent, and treasures–can be shared in many ways.

_____

_____

Pray about what you listed and how you can begin to use the gifts God has given you in the coming months. Write a plan of action, starting with the first step towards that goal. Pray, and re-visit this plan regularly.

_____

_____

Read James 1:17
Dear Lord, please show me in the coming weeks what my gifts are and how You want to use them. I give You my time and talents so You can work to use me to impact others. Help me not focus on just myself and my needs. I don't want to miss where You are working. I love you, Abba Father. Amen.

Day 3

Let's Relate...

Not surprisingly, after the hike down four flights of stairs, my water broke later that night. "I think I wet the bed!" I cried out. I hadn't wet the bed since I was a child, but I had heard that pregnancy could cause strange things. As I sauntered towards the bathroom, I saw a steady stream of water following me. "Yuck!" I exclaimed. I was scared, so I decided it would be better to crawl back in bed and hide to pretend this wasn't happening. That didn't work. When we arrived at the hospital, I looked back to see my water trail. They were putting up caution signs behind me that said, *Careful: Slippery When Wet,* as I made my way to the front desk. How humbling!

An older German nurse named Helga was assigned to me, and she obviously had no patience with first-time moms. Thanks to my HMO medical plan, I was assigned to a doctor I had never met. I now pay extra for a PPO plan.

With my first child, not surprisingly, I was still in labor ten hours later. The baby was ready—however, pushing was a challenge I had not foreseen. The epidural was too strong and caused me to lose all muscle control needed to push. Two hours later, I was still getting yelled at by Helga for not pushing, but I couldn't push. We missed the actual delivery instructions of childbirth because my husband didn't want to miss his favorite TV series to attend our last two classes. There was no fooling Nurse Helga; she could tell immediately we were childbirth class dropouts!

Let's Explore...

1. **Write about a time when someone asked you to do something extremely important. Did you do all of it or just some of what they asked? Why?**

   _____

2. **What is one decision or choice you would change if you could? Have you surrendered that to Christ and are you ready to move forward knowing He already nailed that to the cross.**

   _____

Read Isaiah 41:10 & Lamentations 3:21-25
Dear Lord, help me to be obedient when You ask me to do something. When I struggle, please remind me of Your strength and that You will never leave me or forsake me, as You promise. When I fall, Lord, help me to repent and get back up knowing You have washed me clean, and Your mercies are new every morning. I choose not to remain stagnant Lord. Amen.

Day 4

Let's Relate...

Nurse Helga yelled at me, while the doctor appeared occasionally and said, "You're doing well." I am not naïve and knew I wasn't doing anything well during the horrific labor process. I will take a moment to add here that no book nor person could have adequately prepared me for the process. Meanwhile, I was getting physically sick off the side of the bed while simultaneously hyperventilating. Nurse Helga shoved an oxygen mask over my face. I am claustrophobic, so the mask scared me, but I didn't dare remove it, because at that point I was more afraid of Nurse Helga. I felt smothered, hot, and definitely bothered! After two agonizing hours of pushing (apparently from the neck up instead of the waist down) and my baby being caught in the birth canal by his shoulder, my son came into the world looking like a dark purple plum. "Isn't he beautiful?" Nurse Helga asked. Who would dare disagree with Helga?

"It's finally over," I said, exhausted yet triumphant. "Lay still," my doctor ordered, "I need to deliver the placenta." "Pla, what?" I asked. He described stuff that I must have missed in my pregnancy book, and I made a mental note to ask my mom why she didn't tell me these details. "You mean whatever that is didn't come out with the baby?" I innocently asked. Nurse Helga gave me another one of those looks. Turning towards my husband, I cried, "I knew we should have finished childbirth classes!"

Let's Explore...

1. **Describe what you previously thought of Samson before starting this study.**

   _____

2. **Share a favorite scripture that helps you in difficult situations or circumstances. Why did you choose that particular scripture?**

   _____

Read Isaiah 49:16
Dear Lord, I love that You inscribed me on the palms of Your hands and that Samson nor I was born an accident. You had a plan for Samson and You have a plan for me. I trust You and thank you that You guide me and give me all that I need to fulfill that plan. Amen.

Day 5

Let's Relate...

Meanwhile, out in the waiting room, my mother-in-law heard the baby cry and came barreling through the delivery room yelling, "Where's my grandson?" Nurse Helga immediately charged after my mother-in-law for entering the delivery room without permission. Had I not had my feet stuck in stirrups, I would have followed Nurse Helga to watch her chase my mother-in-law. I would have loved to be a fly on the wall for that encounter! Nurse Helga never returned, and I can only assume it was a great showdown between her and my mother-in-law. She probably met her match and was exhausted after the encounter.

A different nurse came in to explain how I needed to take frequent sitz baths. Another thing my mother didn't tell me. "What in the world is a sitz bath?" I innocently asked. It definitely didn't sound relaxing. The nurse asked, "Can you lift your pelvis?" My pelvis had just gone through many hours of labor, so lifting it was not a welcomed command. If only bodies could talk; I am sure mine would have told me what I could do with such a request. The nurse then shoved a rubber exam glove filled with ice, which looked like a cow udder, underneath me. I decided I needed to write a book that uncovered the real truth about childbirth, and I would spare no detail. In no uncertain terms, I announced in the delivery room, "I am never having sex again!" Like they hadn't heard that one before. Little did I know that exactly three years and one day later, I would be delivering twins and not via cesarean section. Need I remind you how well I do during the pregnancy and labor phases?

Let's Explore...

1. **Spend time thinking about God's plan and promises for your life and share below.**

    _____

2. **Write two steps you can take towards that plan in the next 12 months.**

    _____

Read 2 Timothy 4:7 & Deuteronomy 31:6
Dear Lord, thank you that You enable and equip me to run the race You have for me. I praise You because You never leave my side and I don't have to live in fear. I believe I am who You say I am, I have what You say I can have in Your Word, and I can do what You say I can do. Gently nudge me in the right direction if I begin to run in the wrong lane. I can have courage because of You. I love You Jesus. Amen.

WEEK 2

EMBRACE GOD'S PLAN FOR YOUR LIFE

Last week we learned how Samson moved through the cities unknown, which tells us he didn't physically stand out in a crowd or have lots of muscles, like we might imagine. Another clue that Samson's strength wasn't visible from his outward appearance was that his enemies could never figure out what gave him his strength. Our study begins in the book of Judges, chapter thirteen. A theme we see consistently throughout the Bible is how the Israelites believed in and worshipped God yet would frequently slip back into sinful behavior and ignore God's instruction.

DISCUSS: Can someone give an example of how this pattern of slipping backwards still happens today? Does anyone have insights from last week's lesson to share?

In the Old Testament, God spoke to the people through angels, His chosen prophets, dreams, visions, and even a donkey. In the New Testament, God speaks to us through His Word, Holy Spirit, our consciousness, inner peace, other believers, dreams, visions, situations, and through spiritual authorities such as pastors and leaders.

Let's Dig In...

Read Judges Chapter 13:1-4
Again the children of Israel did evil in the sight of the LORD, and the LORD delivered them into the hand of the Philistines for forty years. Now there was a certain man from Zorah, of the family of the Danites, whose name was Manoah; and his wife who was barren and had no children. And the Angel of the LORD appeared to the woman and said to her, "Indeed now, you are barren and have borne no children, but you shall conceive and bear a son. Now therefore, please be careful not to drink wine or similar drink, and not to eat anything unclean."

Something incredible occurred when an angel of the Lord came to visit Manoah's wife. Scripture does not tell us his wife's name, but we do know the angel brought her good news—after being unable to have a child, she would finally conceive and give birth to a son. What an amazing message! Manoah's wife must have been elated. For many cultures, especially during biblical times, a woman's value was based on her ability to have children, especially sons! The truth is, a woman's worth is based on much more than being able to conceive; God has a plan and a purpose for our lives. The angel of the Lord then gave specific instructions to Manoah's wife to follow precisely during her entire pregnancy.

Read Judges 13:5
"For behold, you shall conceive and bear a son. And no razor shall come upon his head, for the child shall be a Nazarite to God from the womb; and he shall begin to deliver Israel out of the hand of the Philistines."

God's messenger explained to Manoah's wife that her soon-to-be son (Samson) was going to be a Nazarite, which was someone who took a vow to be set apart for God's service. The word Samson means "bright sun," symbolizing that he would be the light for the Israelites against the darkness of their oppression. The book of Judges is a precursor to the book of Kings. In the book of Judges, there was no king yet, because God was the king. Later, the people would demand an earthly king. Notice that the scripture says *he will begin to* deliver his people from the Philistines. It does not say Samson *will* deliver them (as later in scripture King David would do), but that Samson *would be one part* of God's plan.

Read Jeremiah 29:11
"For I know the thoughts that I think towards you," says the Lord, "thoughts of peace and not of evil, to give you a future and a hope."

DISCUSS: God had a plan for Samson, just as He has a plan for each of us. God gives us freedom of choice as to whether we will follow His plan or not. Why is this verse in Jeremiah important? What does this verse about God's plan mean to you personally?

The Hebrew word "Nazar" means separated one. A Nazarite vow was sometimes temporary (six months to a year), but, in Samson's case, it was to be for his entire lifetime. His parents would make the vow for him, and this vow would separate him from the world, as he would be fully dedicated to God. Some denominations have their babies baptized as infants or toddlers and dedicate them to Christ, since they are too young to make the vow themselves.

As a Nazarite, Samson's vow was to be set apart for God, and the outward symbol of this was that he could not cut his hair, touch a dead body, or touch grapes in any form, which included drinking anything containing alcohol.

What did these things symbolize?

- A Nazarite did not cut his hair, because Old Testament scripture says that long hair dishonors a man and brings shame. By having long hair, a Nazarite was willing to bear the shame for the people.
- A Nazarite could not go near or touch anything dead, as he would not be considered clean at that point. Purity was important.
- He could not drink wine, because it is a symbol in scripture of earthly joy, and a Nazarite was to find his joy in God and not in the things around him.

Samson was the twelfth judge of Israel, and twelve is considered a perfect number and the number of authority. Think about the twelve sons of Jacob, who become the twelve tribes of Israel. Remember that Christ had twelve disciples. Samson's purpose was to be an important part of God's plan in delivering Israel from their enemies, the Philistines. The secret of his success was that God had His hand on his life. Samson had amazing strength and abilities when the Spirit of the Lord moved through him.

Most people think Samson's long hair gave him his strength, but this is not the case. His hair was simply a symbol of his covenant with God. A Nazarite was symbolic of a vow made in the person's heart with God. Samson's hair is not the covenant but grew as an outward sign of the covenant in the heart. Have you ever noticed someone filled with the Holy Spirit? Their outward joy and peace are covenant signs with Jesus Christ and show that He lives inside of them.

DISCUSS: What is a symbol of something we wear that would help us understand this covenant point?

The long hair that Samson had was an outer sign of the covenant in his heart, just like a wedding ring is a sign that you are married. A wedding ring is a symbol of marriage, not the actual marriage covenant or relationship itself. A woman can take her wedding ring off, but the fact is, she is still married. Samson's hair was a symbol of his Nazarite vow but not the actual reason he had strength. Even though his hair was simply a symbol, it represented a commitment between him and the Lord, just like marriage is a commitment between you, your husband, and the Lord.

Let me provide some additional historical background. The Lord raised up Samson to deliver Israel from forty years of Philistine oppression. Who were the Philistines? They were enemies of the Israelites and originally came from the island of Crete, arriving at the southern region of Israel. They built five cities and dominated the area for several hundred years. The Philistines were strong, mighty warriors who had multiple advantages, such as more soldiers, better strategy, fighting expertise, and advanced technology—all significant advantages, even in today's times.

The Philistines also controlled and had a monopoly on both iron and blacksmiths, the men who made weapons using iron. On the contrary, the Israelite army had zero iron weapons and even had to go to the Philistines to sharpen their farming tools. Let's take a simple analogy like coffee for a moment. How many of you like coffee or any other caffeinated drink? Let's say there is only one group of people who maintain control of all the coffee in the area.

My mom and I speak at Christian mother/daughter retreats. This requires us to get together frequently to write and prepare. I never needed caffeine to wake up in the morning and didn't start drinking coffee until I was 40 years old and only drink it now for the taste. However, my mom literally can't get moving until she drinks at least two cups of coffee in the morning. When I would arrive at her house after getting my three kids off to school, I could immediately tell whether she'd had her coffee. I knew we wouldn't get any work done if she hadn't! Now, let's imagine the authorities forbid us to have coffee pots in our homes, forcing us to travel to shops run by aggressive, intimidating baristas. There, we have to beg for a cup of coffee, all the while not knowing if they will give us a cup of coffee so we can get our work done.

This seems like a silly comparison, but think about the Israelites who needed to daily work and farm their land to eat, which was common practice during those days. People did not simply run to the neighborhood grocery store to buy groceries. When their farm tools became dull, they had to go to their worst enemy and beg them to sharpen their equipment, so they could simply farm and work. The Philistine knowledge and control over technology, their abundance of weaponry, and their tactical expertise—such as surprise territory raids—greatly terrified and overwhelmed the Israelites. To simplify the vast difference between the two, it was like the Israelites were playing checkers and the Philistines were playing chess.

DISCUSS: Does anyone want to share another example of what this type of oppression would be like today?

What the Philistines had in advantages and weaponry still didn't compare to the Israelites' one advantage: God leading the charge and fighting for Israel. The real challenge was, would the Israelites believe and trust God to go before them? That is the same challenge we face today. Although we may not be concerned with sharpening farm tools, we still have significant obstacles today. Being outsmarted or at a disadvantage doesn't matter in our battles today—battles such as issues with family, health, depression, anxiety, finances, relationships, or work. God wants to go before us and fight our battles, if we surrender our cares to Him (1 Peter 5:7). The question is, will we entrust those cares to a loving Heavenly Father? What really matters is our trusting and being obedient to the Lord, who loves us more than we can imagine. Christ offers us a plan for our lives and walks with us throughout life's journey to carry our burdens, if we let Him.

Read Psalm 55:22
Cast your burden on the Lord, And He shall sustain you; He shall never permit the righteous to be moved.

DISCUSS: Can someone give an example of what Psalm 55:22 means for you personally and how this has played out in your life? What will we do in response to God's love?

- Will we ignore it or embrace it?
- Will we deny it or share it?
- Will we return it or receive it?

When the story of Samson begins, Israel had entered another phase of idolatrous worship. Because God is merciful, He showed grace and raised up a deliverer to help end the trouble, and thus Samson was born. Until that time, the Lord used the Philistines to chasten (discipline) Israel.

DISCUSS: Scripture says God chastens those He loves. What does chasten mean? Anyone want to share a time when they felt like God was lovingly chastening them?

Let's go back to Judges chapter 13, which says that the Lord told Manoah's wife that her son would begin to deliver Israel from the Philistine oppression. Therefore, the mother of Samson was to keep herself holy while she was pregnant, because her son would be set apart for God. This idea of keeping our bodies pure is still present today. Scripture reminds us that our bodies are not our own, and that they belong to Christ.

DISCUSS: Why was it important that Manoah's wife followed God's instructions? What could have happened if she was not obedient?

Read 1 Corinthians 6:19-20
Or do you not know that your body is the temple of the Holy Spirit who is in you, whom you have from God, and you are not your own? For you were bought at a price; therefore glorify God in your body and in your spirit, which are God's.

DISCUSS: Who has heard this verse before? What does the phrase, "bought at a price," mean? Does God still have a plan when we disobey? Can someone give an example of how it might cause a blockade between us, our prayers, and God when we disobey?

Samson's mother was instructed to keep her body pure as part of God's plan. Each person in God's plan has a role and responsibility. When one person doesn't fulfill their responsibility and is disobedient to the Lord, that disrupts His greater plan, as well as causes a rift in our relationship with our creator and Father. Following our role in His plan is the chance for us to show our faith, trust, and obedience to the Lord.

Jesus tells us in the book of John if we love Him, we will obey Him. John 14:15 AMP

DISCUSS: Why is this verse in John a challenge?

Read Judges 13:6-10
So the woman came and told her husband, saying, "A man of God came to me, and His countenance was like the countenance of the Angel of God, very awesome; but I did not ask Him where He was from, and He did not tell me His name. And He said to me, 'Behold, you shall conceive and bear a son. Now drink no wine or similar drink, nor eat anything unclean, for the child shall be a Nazarite to God from the womb to the day of his death.'" Then Manoah prayed to the LORD, and said, "O my Lord, please let the Man of God whom You sent come to us again and teach us what we shall do for the child who will be born." And God listened to the voice of Manoah, and the Angel of God came to the woman again as she sitting in the field; but Manoah her husband was not with her. Then the woman ran in haste and told her husband and said to him, "Look the Man who came to me the other day has just now appeared to me!"

The angel shared instructions for both her pregnancy and for the child who was to be born. Manoah's wife was to make herself holy with her actions and later to share her instructions and obedience with her son Samson. She wouldn't ask her son to do something that she hadn't already done herself. As parents, we are to lead by example until our children can make their faith their own. Manoah then asked the angel to repeat the instructions, and the angel repeated the message.

Read Judges 13:13-14
So the Angel of the Lord said to Manoah, "Of all that I said to the woman let her be careful. She may not eat anything that comes from the vine, nor may she drink wine or similar drink, nor eat anything unclean. All that I commanded her let her observe."

Why did Manoah ask the angel to repeat the instructions? Because they were given to a man! The woman had it down the first time. Although Manoah asked God how He wanted Samson raised, the angel mentioned the role of Manoah's mother. Manoah didn't realize that the issue wasn't the child but the parent. Note that the husband prayed, and the wife got the instructions. God wanted both the man and the woman to be involved in the raising of the child.

Read James 1:22
But be doers of the Word, and not hearers only, deceiving yourselves.

It is not what we say but what we do that matters. The best thing we can do for our children is to maintain our walk with the Lord, so they can observe and do the same. We are to model our faith in action and be doers of the Word. It is not what we say but who we are and what we do that will greatly impact them.

PRAYER REQUESTS AND PRAYER

Individual Reflection Time - Week 2

Day 1

Let's Relate…

As he sat in the swimming pool with a group of my co-workers while on a President's Club sales trip I had won, my new husband, David, had morphed from an introverted, quiet man to a grand storyteller. We were all in the pool, and my co-workers, who I had known for years, gathered around waiting to hear about how we had met, since I had always kept my private life separate from business discussions.

Slowly, I watched as my co-workers formed a circle around David during his story, and I found myself on the outside of the crowd. He came alive in a way I had never seen as he began to describe when we first met and how reticent I had been about commitment. Everyone was shocked, because I am such an outgoing, friendly, and approachable person. What they didn't know is due to a painful childhood and difficult divorce after 17 years of marriage, I avoided getting close to someone. The crowd got larger as more came over from their lounge chairs on the side of the pool and joined the others to listen.

Let's Explore…

1. **A woman can have a tremendous impact when she remains calm and soothing, especially to her husband, family, or friends. Describe a time when you remained calm in an unusual, frightening, or confusing situation.**

   _____

2. **How have you been able to help others during these situations, or is it someone else that usually helps you?**

   _____

Read Isaiah 26:3
Dear Lord, I will not let fear, nervousness, or anxiety control me. I know You can help me to remain calm in ALL situations and know You are God, and You are on the throne. Remind me that You fill me with Your amazing peace so that others will take note of my disposition and know it comes from You. I cling to Your promise in Isaiah, and I praise You and trust You.

Day 2

Let's Relate...

David continued the story and shared that after four months of dating, he was falling in love with me. What David hadn't known was I could tell by his eyes that he was falling in love, and I knew the words would soon escape his lips. I became nervous and decided to make a move and fast to avoid hurting such a wonderful man.

David continued the story as my co-workers stared wide-eyed at him and then back at me, now squeezed to the outside of the circle. Being extroverted, I quickly tried to intercede and tell my side of the story, since these were my co-workers. I just knew they would listen. Unbeknownst to me, they wanted to hear David's account and moved to close the circle once again around him. I didn't know what to do. I had always been the presenter and the center of attention. Didn't they want to hear my side of the story?

Let's Explore...

1. **Think of a time in your life when you felt someone had an advantage over you such as the Philistines?**

   _____

2. **How did this impact you, and what did you do to persevere even though you felt like everything was against you?**

   _____

Read Psalm 139:7-10
Dear Lord, remind me of Your promises and how You go before me, and it doesn't matter what anyone may say or do – You hold me in Your mighty right hand as You promise. The battle is won, and You are the victor, and I will trust this situation and this person to You. When I'm not trusting You, help me to remember that I am mistakenly taking control back. This action says You are not big enough to handle my situations and I know that's not true. Thank you for forgiving me Father. Amen.

Day 3

Let's Relate…

David continued to share to the crowd, "So the next thing I know, out of the blue, Diana breaks up with me." They were all shocked that I would break up with such a great guy after they had gotten to know him on this trip. Heads turned to finally notice me and watch for my response. I have an uncontrollable habit that I have had since I was a child, which is laughing when I'm nervous or upset. It's an inappropriate habit and always surfaces at the wrong moment. My coworkers watched for my response, and what did I do next? I broke into laughter. Aghast, they really crowded me out to focus on David, who seemed to be the sensible, calm one.

"I can't believe she would just break up with you for no reason," my closest co-worker exclaimed. "Yes, and she broke up via email," David added. Shocked, they parted the circle just enough to see my reaction. Of course, I could only smile to keep from bursting out laughing due to my nervous habit. It sounded so much worse hearing it from the lips of my dear husband. I tried to explain, but who would understand my reasons and that it was an irrational response that caused me to react in a way to protect myself from commitment? I knew better than anyone that my response was not justifiable, and, at that early point in our relationship, David wasn't aware of my painful past.

Let's Explore…

1. **Name a time when you had to wait for something or someone and it was extremely challenging because things weren't happening the way you had in mind?**

   _____

2. **What made it so hard and what was the outcome?**

   _____

Read Hebrews 13:8
Dear Lord, I know You always have a plan and a purpose and that while I am waiting, You are always working. Help me trust You and Your plan for my life in all situations, no matter what that plan looks like. You are the same God yesterday, today, and forever as You tell me in Your Word in Hebrews. Remind me of Your presence and love in a tangible way. Amen.

Day 4

Let's Relate…

"But she did call me back," David was quick to jump in as my defense. They all seem relieved that I would eventually do the right thing. "Nine months later," David added and laughed. Now, I will confess that I was not the quickest to admit I was wrong. It took me some time to process, allow myself to absorb the situation, and then to decide on next steps—otherwise known as stubbornness or pride. Most of the time, I just ignored or ran from difficult issues, and then I didn't have to think about them, which prevented me from being upset or uncomfortable.

The good news is the Lord is faithful, and He is always beside me, constantly refining my character. God continued to penetrate my spirit to remind me of how I could always trust Him, and that I shouldn't live in fear and continue running from difficult situations. Soon after, I spent weeks being able to think of nothing but David and knew it was from the Lord. I knew I had to call and apologize for my behavior and offer closure. I didn't know the Lord had planned on reconciliation and that David was who He had in mind for me to later marry. I just knew God wanted me to be obedient and call to apologize.

Let's Explore…

1. **Name a time when you cried out to God and He answered, but it wasn't in the way you wanted.**

   _____

2. **Looking back, what did you learn from what you asked for and how God may have put something different into motion?**

   _____

Read Hebrews 13:5b-6
Dear Lord, I admit I can't always understand why some things happen and why some people do what they do. It is in the surrender of understanding where I can begin to trust You and let You have control of my life. When I try to get control back from You, gently remind me that Your ways are higher. Help me let go of pride, stubbornness, and insistence of an outcome that I can understand because You are my helper as You promise. Amen.

Day 5

Let's Relate...

The phone call to David was not easy for me. After a week of wrestling with the Lord, I knew I needed to obey, and I resolutely picked up the phone. Because so much time had passed, David was surprised to hear my voice. I let him know that the Lord had been working on me, and I needed to apologize for the way I'd ended our relationship. He forgave me, and, after a few minutes of conversation and catching up, we hung up the phone. A few minutes later, the phone rang again, and David asked if we could meet for dinner to further discuss my call, so I agreed. It was the least I could do to provide closure.

Anxiously, I waited across the street from the restaurant where we had agreed to meet. And then I saw David walking towards me from the other direction. It was good to see him. We had a nice dinner, and, afterwards, he walked me to my car and asked if we could try again. Even though I did want to continue to see him, I didn't want to hurt him again. I knew I needed to explain that I wasn't sure if I was capable of commitment or a relationship. Furthermore, I was busy at work, writing a book, and caring for my three kids, and didn't have much time to date. "We have to take it very slow," I cautioned. Basically, I was warning David not to tell me he loved me or push me to say the same anytime soon. I knew in time I would need to acknowledge and share my past with David, so he could understand my trepidation. We were engaged a year later. My husband always says, "It's not how you start, but how you finish."

Let's Explore...

1. **Share a time when you asked something specific from the Lord.**

   _____

2. **What is the hardest part of waiting for God's reply? How has He used that in your spiritual development?**

   _____

Read Psalm 18:30
Dear Lord, it's hard when I struggle to hear You correctly, or You don't answer me in the way I would choose. Help me to trust that You always have a plan and know what is best for me because You love me as Your Word states. You are more concerned with my character than my comfort. Help me to follow Your lead and walk in Your ways. Amen.

WEEK 3

TRUSTING THE LORD WITH HIS GIFTS

DISCUSS: Would anyone like to share from your reflection time this past week?

Let's Dig In…

Read Judges 13:17
Then Manoah said to the Angel of the Lord, "What is Your name, that when Your words come to pass we may honor you?"

Manoah wanted to know the angel's name, so he could honor him when his message became reality. The angel refused and replied that Manoah wouldn't understand it. Manoah was more focused on the messenger and his name than on the fact that he and his wife were receiving specific instructions from the Lord Almighty. Manoah also wanted to give an offering, so he asked the angel to stay while he prepared a sacrifice. Offerings are a sign of honor, respect, and worship. This was Manoah's way of telling the Lord he would be obedient and serve Him through his actions.

DISCUSS: In this case, Manoah was wanting to give honor to the messenger. Sometimes we focus more on the messenger instead of their message. Why?

Read Judges 13:20
Scripture tells us that Manoah and his wife watched as the alter flame burned upward toward heaven, and the angel of the Lord ascended into the flame. Manoah and his wife fell on their faces to the ground.

I think I would also fall to my face on the ground if an angel rose into a flame above my head. In the New Testament, Christ rose into a cloud in front of His disciples. Much of the Old Testament is foreshadowing the New Testament and Christ's coming.

Read Judges 13:22-23
Manoah, realizing it was an angel of the Lord, tells his wife in panic, "We shall surely die, because we have seen God." But his wife said to him, "If the LORD had desired to kill us, He would not have accepted a burnt offering and a grain offering from our hands, nor would He have shown us all these things, nor would He have told us such things as these at this time."

Throughout the narrative, Manoah's wife remained calm and sensible. The angel never appeared again. Our serenity and disposition with our husband can have a profound impact on his demeanor, as well as others around us. I once heard a radio interview where the DJ asked the wife of a well-known and popular evangelist how she kept her husband humble. The wife responded that her job was not to keep her husband humble—that was God's job. Her job was to pray, support, and encourage her husband. How often do we focus on letting God do His work? Sometimes, I make the mistake of thinking God needs my help removing flaws in my husband.

Read Matthew 7:3
And why do you look at the speck in your brother's eye but do not consider the plank in your own eye?

When we step out of the way and let God lead both us and our husband, we can remain calm and lay our fears, burdens, and our need to control our circumstances at the foot of the cross. What a witness for both our husband and others. Know what we bring to the table as women, but also know the Lord wants to be Lord of our lives, and we need to follow His leading so His plan is revealed in us.

DISCUSS: Do you think the calmness of Manoah's wife was a typical response upon seeing an angel? Why do you think she was able to remain calm? Why is our disposition and response to the men (husbands, fathers, sons, brothers) in our lives important? What can we as women provide?

Read Judges 13:24-25
So the woman bore a son and called his name Samson; and the child grew, and the Lord blessed him. And the Spirit of the Lord began to move upon him at Mahaneh Dan, between Zorah and Eshtaol.

DISCUSS: What does the *Spirit of the Lord began to move upon him* mean?

Mahaneh Dan was a city between Zorah and Eshtaol, several miles west of Jerusalem, that belonged to the tribe of Dan and bordered the tribe of Judah. God impressed upon Samson's heart the difficulties of his tribe and began to stir supernaturally in him. The Spirit aroused in Samson a desire to serve God for his people's deliverance and was God's way of prompting him to take action when needed.

God empowered Samson to deliver Israel but not by leading the Israelites against the Philistines, as King David would later do in scripture. Samson performed his exploits alone and helped the Israelites by disrupting and inhibiting Philistine invasions. Samson's strength was not in his arms or body or even hair. The secret of his strength was in the *Spirit of God* upon him. When the Spirit moved in Samson, no one could stop him, because he was displaying God's incredible power through his abilities.

God works the same way through us. Perhaps there are times you feel a stir in your heart or spirit. This stir may indicate an area where God wants to use you. Pray about these stirrings, and ask the Lord to show you what they mean and how He wants to use you as part of His greater plan. Remember that the Lord doesn't typically reveal His entire plan at once, but usually gives us one step at a time as a lesson in faith, trust, and obedience. Ask Christ for your next step. Confirm with scripture what you think He is telling you. Anything you receive from another person or that you feel comes from the Lord will never contradict His Word. Ask God where He is working and how you can join Him. The will of God won't take you where the grace of God won't keep you.

DISCUSS: Are there are things that are stirring in your heart or spirit? Can you think of a time when God gave you just one step in His plan? What does it mean when it says the Spirit will never contradict His Word?

Dear Lord, please show me where are You working and how I can join You. How may I be the hands and feet of Christ? What is the next step You would have me take? Give me eyes to see and ears to hear when You are calling me, and help me to be obedient when I receive Your call.

Read 2 Samuel 22:31
As for God, His way is perfect; The word of the Lord is proven; He is a shield to all who trust in Him.

God asks us to trust Him and be obedient to His Word. Samson's mother and father were obedient to the Word of the Lord and the instructions sent by the angel. God uses a variety of means to develop and prepare us: hereditary traits, environmental influences, and personal experiences. As with Samson, this preparation often begins long before adulthood. Work to be sensitive to the Holy Spirit's leading and the plan God has ordained for you. Your past may be more useful than you imagine. The experiences you have been through can be a significant source of strength, hope, and encouragement for those who are currently going through similar situations or for those who may go through them later in life.

DISCUSS: How can we be sensitive to God's Spirit? How are your experiences a source of strength or encouragement for others? Do you think people want a comforting word from someone who has been through a similar experience? Why or why not?

Read Judges 14:1-2
Now Samson went down to Timnah and saw a woman in Timnah of the daughters of the Philistines. So he went up and told his father and mother, "I have seen a woman in Timnah of the daughters of the Philistines; now therefore, get her for me as a wife."

These are Samson's first recorded words in the Bible, and they are important, because it is obvious that it was a woman's beauty that caught his eye—even though it was a woman from the enemy tribe. His demand also shows his lack of respect for God's plan for his life and for his parents. He wanted what he wanted. This relationship was discouraged, because he was an Israelite, and because he was set apart for God. This began the tangled weave of Samson's downfall—lust of his eyes and later his obsession for women.

Another Bible version says, *"She looked good to him so Samson ordered his parents to take her."* If I was Samson's mother, I am not sure how I would respond to his demand. His comments are disturbing, not to mention extremely disrespectful and demanding of his parents. It was obvious, at least initially, that he only wanted her because of her beauty, since they had never met nor spoken. In these few recorded words, Samson showed his weakness—wanting a woman even if she didn't know or worship the Lord God.

DISCUSS: After seeing the foreign woman in a field, did he want her for her personality, virtuousness, intelligence, or kindness? Do we as women look at more than outward appearances when searching for a husband? Have you pre-determined what is most important to you? Does your list include a man after God's own heart?

His father and mother asked him to reconsider and find a wife among his relatives. This is also disturbing for different reasons but is typical of how things were handled in that day. Marriage negotiations were customarily handled by the parents and kept within the family bloodlines. Samson's parents referred to the Philistines as uncircumcised. Per Mosaic law, an Israelite was not permitted to marry someone outside of their religion, and his parents did not want him marrying a Philistine wife from amongst their enemies. They tried to warn him not to be yoked with an unbeliever.

Read 2 Corinthians 6:14-15
Do not be unequally yoked together with unbelievers. For what fellowship has righteousness with lawlessness? And what communion has light with darkness? And what accord has Christ with Belial? Or what part has a believer with an unbeliever?

Samson wanting a woman who did not worship the Lord showed his disobedience and disrespect of both God and his parents. Part of being unequally yoked was the Lord warning Samson and believers past, present, and future not to be involved with the dead things of the world (saved versus unsaved). Because Samson was a Nazarite, he was to keep away from death and decay. This didn't just mean dead animals and people but those in spiritual death.

DISCUSS: What does unequally yoked mean? Why is it important? What can happen to a believer in this circumstance, whether dealing with marriage or your closest inner circle of friends?

Read Amos 3:3
Can two walk together unless they are agreed? (Message version: Do two people walk hand in hand if they aren't going to the same place?)

Proverbs 12:26
The righteous should choose his friends carefully, for the way of the wicked leads them astray.

Because He made us, the Lord knows how fragile our faith and obedience is. When we choose a spouse or have a best friend who isn't a believer, God knows the chance of them pulling us away from Him is far greater than we imagine. God knows our heart, and, even if we are a positive influence in their life, they can still lead us astray.

Jesus teaches us to love others and be a witness in our actions to those around us. However, concerning our closest inner circle of friends or a spouse, we are instructed in 2 Corinthians 6:14-15 and Amos 3:3 that our inner circle of friends and our spouse should be believers and have hearts to follow the Lord.

DISCUSS: If married: What is the importance of being in one accord with your spouse?
If single: Determine a list of traits you want in a man before you begin dating. This will prevent swaying values due to emotions and feelings that can be blinding in the initial days and months of dating.

Read Judges 14:3
Then his father and mother said to him, "Is there no woman among the daughters of your brethren, or among all my people, that you must go and get a wife from the uncircumcised Philistines?" And Samson said to his father, "Get her for me for she pleases me well."

Not only was Samson an Israelite, but he was a Nazarite devoted to God, and he was choosing to be with a woman who worshiped an idol, the Philistine's god, Dagon. We read that Samson's heroic demonstrations of physical strength and prowess with the Philistines began at the time of his impending marriage to a Philistine woman.

Read Judges 14:5-6a
So Samson went down to Timnah with his father and mother, and came to the vineyards of Timnah. Now to his surprise, a young lion came roaring against him. And the Spirit of the Lord came mightily upon him, and he tore the lion apart as one would have torn apart a young goat, though he had nothing in his hand.

As you recall, Samson was supposed to stay away from grapes, so he had no business being near a vineyard. Judges 14:5-6 goes on to describe Samson's journey to Timnah with his parents, when a young lion came roaring towards him. Remember, he was in a place where he shouldn't have been when he came face to face with an enemy. You may have heard of this account, which is told frequently in children's Bible stories and was made into a children's song. Scripture says, "the *Spirit of the Lord came mightily upon him*," and Samson tore the lion apart with his bare hands.

Read 1 Peter 5:8
Be sober, be vigilant; because your adversary the devil walks about like a roaring lion, seeking whom he may devour.

DISCUSS: Was Samson supposed to be in Timnah? What happened to the lion and why? Who is the lion compared to in 1 Peter 5:8?

When scripture refers to the Spirit of the Lord coming upon him in power, it refers to the unusual physical strength the Lord gave Samson. Now, Samson may have been missing a few things in the noggin, but he definitely had strength. Satan is compared in scripture to a roaring lion. Many times, the lions in our lives come dressed in sheep's clothing, which is how Satan finds an opening into our lives.

By enabling Samson to kill a lion (the enemy) with his bare hands, God was displaying His power through Samson, so he would realize he didn't have to be afraid to face even the biggest difficulties and battles in life. God is always preparing us for battle with the enemy, whether we realize it or not. Jesus came to live inside of us so that we would have His Holy Spirit's strength and the victory through Him.

PRAYER REQUESTS AND PRAYER

Individual Reflection Time - Week 3

Day 1

Let's Relate...

I woke up from my back surgery groggy and in immense pain. Through my blurry vision, I looked down and appeared to have white, thigh-high hose on each leg. Where was I? Was this a dream? I had seen these thigh highs in lingerie stores but always in a package or on a mannequin and never on the lower half of my body. I must admit they looked better on the mannequin. Being 5'3" and having thick thighs, when I wrestled to put a tight elastic band around my thigh, all that flesh was forced to travel somewhere. When pushed up and over the thigh-high band, it didn't make for an attractive fashion statement or romantic image! I tried to focus and glanced around the room and finally saw my husband and realized...it was not date night!

Let's Explore...

1. **Share a time when you saw either someone or something you wanted and didn't want to take *"No"* as an answer from either God, your parents, or other influencers in your life.**

   _____

2. **What was the outcome, and would you do things differently now?**

   _____

Read Psalm 103:11-12
Dear Lord, I come to You with my past mistakes and ask You to forgive me. I am confident that as I confess my sins, You are faithful to forgive as You say in Psalms. Show me how to forgive myself. Nudge me in the right direction when I go places or do things that are not according to Your will and get me back on Your path of righteousness. I praise You Lord. Amen.

Day 2

Let's Relate...

I looked from my husband across the room and saw a doctor and remembered I had gone in for surgery earlier that morning. Realizing these thigh highs weren't a gift from my husband, and it wasn't Valentine's Day, I immediately asked the doctor, "What are these?" Apparently having heard that question too many times before from patients, he sarcastically challenged, "If you don't want to have a blood clot, you will wear them. It is up to you if you want the clot or not." So much for bedside manner. He was not charming and had no patience for hearing my opinion. For a fleeting moment, I thought, *Maybe I can pull this thigh-high thing off and appear sexy for a few days!* I quickly snapped back to reality and blamed that thought on the effects of the anesthesia and realized these thigh highs were a regrettable necessity.

Let's Explore...

1. **Describe a time when you felt the Holy Spirit stirring within you.**

   _____

2. **How did you feel or respond?**

   _____

Read Psalm 37:34
Dear Lord, help me recognize when Your spirit is stirring within me and not to miss what You are trying to do. Work through me Lord to be obedient to Your will and walk in Your ways. My hope will always be in You since You are the Alpha and Omega, the First and the Last. You promise that my hope is secure in You, and You will exalt me, and I will inherit the land You have for me. I receive that promise. Amen.

Day 3

Let's Relate...

Because my surgery was done via laser, I was able to return to work quickly. However, I still had to wear the circulation hose around the clock. The white thigh highs looked glaringly obvious! Why don't they make these things in black? I was late for a meeting and began hurrying down the hall, when I felt something pop on my right thigh. I didn't have time to investigate, as this was an important meeting, and I had to be on time, but, as I walked in, people were staring at my skirt and then down to my ankle. The hose on my right leg had quickly slid from the top of my thigh all the way down to my ankle. So, that was the noise I heard. So much for professionalism at the office. It definitely wouldn't make for a romantic evening later with my husband either.

Let's Explore...

1. **Did you ever give excessive attention to something or someone you shouldn't have?**

    _____

2. **If so, what did you decide to do going forward to prevent that from happening again?**

    _____

Read 1 Corinthians 10:13
Dear Lord, thank you that You always give me a way out of situations that I shouldn't be in as Your Word promises in 1 Corinthians. Give me wisdom to know when I am headed the wrong direction and courage to turn quickly before I find myself in a dead-end. Thank you for Your love, faithfulness, and forgiveness when I repent. Amen.

Day 4

Let's Relate...

How embarrassing! I couldn't reach down and grab and adjust my hose in front of all those people. I think everyone understood when I excused myself to go to the restroom and fix the situation. I didn't realize it was hopeless at the time. As I walked back to the meeting, I had to continually grab the top of my hose and pull as hard as I could to hide it under my skirt before it fell all the way back down to my ankle again. Without elastic, it lasted for about three steps before it slid back down to my knee and continued south. I even tried walking with a "step with my left leg and drag with my right leg" approach. No such luck.

Let's Explore...

1. **Describe a time when you were quick to make a judgement call and later found out you were wrong.**

    _____

2. **How did that impact you and was it difficult to correct the situation?**

    _____

Read James 1:19-20
Dear Lord, You are a merciful God. Sometimes, I assume things I shouldn't or am too quick to speak or act when time and understanding is what's needed. Give me Your wisdom to do the right thing and take the time to turn everything over to You in prayer. Amen.

Day 5

Let's Relate...

Taking the pantyhose off in the reception area was not an option. So once again, I yanked the hose from the outside of my skirt while trying to be as professional as possible. Surely, no one was really paying attention. By the time I made it back to the meeting room entrance, my one thigh high was around my right ankle again. You can imagine the thoughts of those seated around the table, as they had seen the whole thing through the glass conference room doors. I stood up straight, held my head high, threw my shoulders back, and walked in confidently to take my seat as if nothing had happened. That would teach them to stare!

Let's Explore...

1. **Who is your closest friend? What do you like most about them?**

   _____

2. **Who has been your biggest challenge to get along with either from your past, or presently?**

   _____

3. **What has God shown or taught you through the relationships you mentioned above?**

   _____

Read Proverbs 13:20
Dear Lord, please help me to inquire of You concerning my choice of a mate and who my closest inner circle of friends should be. Proverbs 13:20 says, "Walk with the wise and become wise, for a companion of fools suffers harm." When I seek You first in all things, You give me wisdom and discernment to make wise decisions. Gently remind me when I forget to bring matters to You and seek Your direction. Amen.

WEEK 4

SAMSON'S OWN STORYTELLING EMERGES

DISCUSS: Anyone want to share about their reflection time this past week?

Let's Dig In...

At the end of week two, we ended with God providing the strength and power for Samson to kill the lion with only his bare hands. God wants to give us His strength and power, if we will receive it.

Read Judges 14:7
Then he went down and talked with the woman; and she pleased Samson well.

What a day for Samson—first defeating a wild beast, then having his first conversation with a beautiful woman and deciding she was the one to be his wife. Things were much simpler back then.

Read Judges 14:8-9
After some time, when he returned to get her, he turned aside to see the carcass of the lion. And behold, a swarm of bees and honey were in the carcass of the lion. He took some of it in his hands and went along, eating. When he came to his father and mother, he gave some to them, and they also ate. But he did not tell them that he had taken the honey out of the carcass of the lion.

Scripture tells us that some time passed before Samson went back to marry the woman from Timnah, and, along his journey, he ran across the lion that he had previously killed. The carcass had a swarm of bees, so he scooped out some honey and ate it as he walked along. It is important to note at this point in the story that Samson had violated his Nazarite vow, because, when he scooped honey from the lion's carcass, he had to touch the lion's dead body to get the honey. Samson knew he was violating a Nazarite vow, because it says in verse nine that he didn't tell his parents where he got the honey. Remember, one of the conditions of being a Nazarite was that Samson could not touch anything dead.

DISCUSS: Why didn't he tell his parents where he got the honey? Why do we sometimes hide information from those around us? Do you notice that Samson is continually violating his vows? How might this be like us in our daily choices?

Read Luke 11:28
But He said, "More than that, blessed are those who hear the word of God and keep it!"

DISCUSS: What does the verse in Luke mean to you? Whose strength is always available to us even when we are in places we shouldn't be (Timnah)?

We are to daily seek God's Spirit in our lives. When we pray and the enemy tries to come at us during the day, we can call upon God's Spirit for strength, even when we are in places we shouldn't be. When we wait to pray until later, we are tackling the day in our own strength. Our strength requires a daily dependence upon God, because, on our own, we are not powerful enough to defeat the enemy and handle many of life's daily challenges.

Later in the story, as Samson was preparing for his wedding, he threw a customary seven-day feast for thirty companions, and at this feast they drank wine. This violated another Nazarite vow, which was to not let alcohol touch his lips. Typically, this feast would occur in the groom's home, and Samson would've had Israelite companions. However, because his bride was from Timnah and not his hometown of Zorah, Samson was at her home to throw the feast. Because he was at her home, his companions were from the enemy tribe. This wasn't your average bachelor party. Because Samson was far from home, he needed wedding attendants. You can imagine that the Philistine companions assigned to him for the ceremony didn't like him or the fact that they were forced to be his attendants.

DISCUSS: What do feasts typically serve? Does this break his vow as a Nazarite? Is it easy to see and find fault with Samson for his many mistakes? Why is it sometimes easier to recognize bad choices in others rather than see them in ourselves?

First, Samson was in the vineyard, where he shouldn't have been because of the grapes, and then, shortly after that, he touched the dead lion's body. Lastly, he throws a party, which, according to Philistine custom, was more like a drunken brawl. Three strikes at this point for Samson. Remember that Samson's wedding attendants were enemies because he was getting married in a foreign city where his wife lived.

Read Judges 14:12-13
Then Samson said to them, "Let me pose a riddle to you. If you can correctly solve and explain it to me within the seven days of the feast, then I will give you thirty linen garments and thirty

sets of clothing. But if you cannot explain it to me, then you shall give me thirty linen garments and thirty changes of clothing." And they said to him, "Pose your riddle that we may hear it."

Normally, the groom bought gifts for his groomsmen, but Samson didn't want to buy gifts for these thirty men, so he told them a riddle as a way to get out of having to purchase anything for them. This wasn't a fun riddle, where Samson was horsing around with close friends, but a way for Samson to taunt and frustrate his enemies. In his naturally smug manner, Samson told his thirty companions the riddle.

Read Judges 14:14
So he said to them, "Out of the eater came something to eat, And out of the strong came something sweet." Now for three days they could not explain the riddle.

DISCUSS: Many times, joking has a mean streak behind it with an agenda. What is usually the result of this type of joking?

There was no way for his enemies to solve the riddle, since they weren't in the field when he killed the lion and ate the honey from the dead carcass. As time passed, the Philistines still couldn't decipher the riddle, so they went to Samson's wife and persuaded her to use her influence to get him to explain the riddle. To ensure her compliance, they said if she didn't agree to coax her husband into confessing how to solve the riddle, they would burn her and her father's household to death. Imagine—these were her people. What a savory group of folks.

Read Judges 14:16a; 17a
Then Samson's wife wept on him, and said, "You only hate me! You do not love me! You have posed a riddle to the sons of my people, but you have not explained it to me..." Now she had wept on him the seven days while their feast lasted...

Wow, what drama, and not much of a wedding feast or celebration. His new wife continued to pressure him day after day. A woman's most powerful weapon can be tears, pouting, or the cold shoulder, and Samson's wife turned on the water works for seven straight days. Sometimes women can be masters at getting their way, especially using tears. Does it work? Amazingly enough, many times it does.

DISCUSS: Have you ever done something similar? If so, did you achieve your objective? Do you think this type of pressure is effective? Why or why not?

Not surprisingly, Samson finally broke down after many days of his wife's tears and begging and explained the riddle on the seventh day. What did his wife do with the information? Of course, she immediately ran to her people, and, before sunset, his enemies proudly solved the riddle.

Obviously, Samson was extremely angry when he realized his own wife had betrayed him. This wasn't the only time in Samson's life that a woman would betray him. It is important to note that this event was a turning point for Samson and would haunt and consume him the rest of his life.

Read Judges 14:18
So the men of the city said to him on the seventh day before the sun went down: "What is sweeter than honey? And what is stronger than a lion?" And he [Samson] said to them, "If you had not plowed with my heifer, you would not have solved my riddle!"

To be referred to as a heifer would have thrown me into another seven-day sob fest.

Read Judges 14:19a
Then the Spirit of the Lord came down upon him mightily…

Notice the mention again of the phrase, "Then the Spirit of the Lord." Despite Samson's pride, foolishness, and games, the Lord still empowered him with His Spirit for the purpose of humbling the Philistines and disrupting their domination of the Israelites. God has a plan, and, even when we make the wrong choices, He still seeks to accomplish that plan.

In Samson's anger at his enemies solving his riddle and his wife's lack of allegiance, he traveled to the neighboring city, Ashkelon, and killed thirty of their men. Samson stripped them of their belongings and gave their clothes to the men who solved the riddle. Why did he do this? Because Samson didn't want his hand forced into having to purchase garments for his enemies, whom he despised. In his fury, he then left town to go to his father's house to let his anger subside.

Samson had every right to be angry both at his wife and his enemies. However, we must remember Samson lit the fire with an unsolvable riddle intended to trick and mock his enemies. Additionally, no one forced Samson to marry a woman who was from an enemy tribe and not from amongst his own people. He disobeyed and brought contention upon himself yet was surprised when the Philistines turned around to trick him.

We need to look at our part in situations. We have a choice in how we should respond, even when wronged by others. God is more concerned with our character than our comfort. Scripture says that we are to leave vengeance to the Lord and trust Him with those who harm us.

Read Romans 12:19
Beloved, do not avenge yourselves, but rather give place to wrath, for it is written; "Vengeance is Mine; I will repay," says the Lord.

DISCUSS: Revenge is a powerful thing, manifesting in anger and retaliation. Anyone willing to share a time you acted immediately in revenge? How might it have helped to wait to until your anger subsided and spent that time in prayer instead?

Back at Samson's wife's home, how did her father respond? He assumed Samson was so angry that he wouldn't want to be with his wife anymore, so his father-in-law gave her to his wedding companion (best man). Our husband is our spiritual covering. Even though she didn't know the God, Samson did, and, had she trusted her husband with her dilemma, he could have prayed, and God would have intervened. Instead, she didn't trust or confide in her new husband, and went and plotted with her own people in fear of their death threat. His wife's allegiance should have been to her husband first before her family or people, as this is God's command once married.

DISCUSS: God has a plan for our allegiance—God is first, our husband is second, and then our children and/or family are third. When we mix up the order, we are removing our spiritual covering and inviting dilemma into our lives. Is this order a struggle? Is it more challenging when children are involved? Why or why not?

Read Judges 15:1a
After a while, in the time of wheat harvest, it happened that Samson visited his wife with a young goat.

During Samson's time, they had the type of marriage where arrangements were made directly with the bride's family. The wife continued to live at home with her father, and her husband visited her periodically. Now, this might be quite nice. You have plenty of alone time and don't have to share the toothpaste tube or put the toilet seat down, but you get a few fun visits here and there. Because some time had passed since the drama with the riddle, Samson's anger had subsided towards his wife, so he got a young goat and went to visit her. I'm thinking, bring me a shiny new bracelet, flowers, chocolate, or a love letter—not a goat. But to each their own.

Read Judges 15:1b-2
And he said, "Let me go in to my wife, into her room." But her father would not permit him to go in. Her father said, "I really thought that you thoroughly hated her; therefore I gave her to your companion. Is not her younger sister better than she? Please take her instead."

Now that is an in-law story to share around the water cooler at work! I don't even know where to begin with her father's suggestion of trading his youngest daughter for his eldest daughter as a quick fix. It's a good thing I didn't live back then—my comments would have gotten me beheaded.

In those days, the word that her father used, hate, was a technical term used in the context of divorce, so, when Samson returned, his father-in-law assumed he had divorced his daughter. Samson's temper was boiling at this point—he hadn't known his wife had been given to another man. No man back then (or today) wants to share his wife. One can imagine how Samson must have felt—one betrayal after another. Realizing the serious misunderstanding and mistake, his father-in-law quickly tried to barter with Samson by offering his younger, more attractive daughter.

He had been betrayed by his wife with the riddle, and then his father-in-law gave her to another man. Samson became extremely angry and would have issues with women from that day forward. He continued in lust for women with his eyes—not wanting to open himself up and be vulnerable to God's blessing of true love but seeking instead to protect himself. From that point on, Samson developed an attitude and defense mechanism that affected the rest of his life.

DISCUSS: How might wounds from the past affect our current attitude and reactions?

Samson continued to look back at what was done to him and how his trust was betrayed instead of looking forward and clinging to God's faithfulness. When we are focused on looking back at our past, we are unable to see what God has for us in the future. We allow past experiences to consume us and dictate how we move forward in life. This can occur with any painful experience or unmet expectation, not just a marriage. Maybe you were treated unfairly or harshly at work or by a parent or sibling. If we aren't careful to lay these painful experiences at the foot of the cross, before we know it, we realize we are carrying them with us, and the load is more than we can bear.

Read Matthew 11:28
Come to Me, all you who labor and are heavy laden, and I will give you rest.

Samson believed he was fighting in the name of the Lord, but he was fighting by his own flesh out of hurt and anger.

DISCUSS: Do we sometimes do the same and claim it's in the name of the Lord?

Do we say we have forgiven others when we haven't, which results in not only holding others but ourselves hostage? Maybe we don't forgive ourselves, so we hang on to our own mistakes and let this negative focus pull us in a direction we don't want to go. Samson should have laid his burdens down and trusted God to avenge those who hurt him. Betrayal consumed him, and the Philistines became aware of his weakness—women.

Read Judges Chapter 15:3-5
And Samson said to them, "This time I shall be blameless regarding the Philistines if I harm them!" Then Samson went and caught three hundred foxes; and he took torches, turned the foxes tail to tail, and put a torch between each pair of tails. When he had set the torches on fire, he let the foxes go into the standing grain of the Philistines, and burned up both the shocks and the standing grain, as well as the vineyards and the olive groves.

The Philistines were extremely angry at the damage to their crops. They asked around to find out who had caused the fire that destroyed their fields, and it didn't take long to receive the answer. They were told it was Samson, because his wife was given to another man. The Philistines were livid and immediately went and got Samson's father-in-law and wife and burned them both to death.

Again, I'm glad I didn't live back then. These were their own people, and they were killed because of property damage to crops. So much needless suffering occurred because of pride and revenge. If only Samson had not let his anger control him. Instead of being angry at his wife and walking out on her, Samson could have forgiven her. How different things might have been.

DISCUSS: A lot of suffering took place that could have been prevented if Samson had not let his anger control him. What could have happened if he had shown his wife mercy, kindness, and forgiveness?

Samson married into the very people who were his enemies. This is indicative of the inner fight within us between our spirit and our flesh. We are at war with things that attract us, such as lust, obsession, money, and greed. We don't like that we covet, yet we do it anyway. We don't like that we lust, yet we do it anyway. We are at war with what we want but isn't good for us, and this is a constant battle between our flesh and spirit.

His wife's people had said they would kill her if she didn't find the answer to Samson's riddle. Instead of having allegiance to her husband, she manipulated others to protect herself and try to prevent her death. She sought to work a deal with her people against her husband, but, in the end, they turned on her and not only killed her but also her father. Samson's wife died, because she didn't honor God or her husband and bartered with the enemy. What's sad about this story is that his wife tried to protect herself from being burned when they initially threatened her, yet, when she betrayed her husband, she set into motion events that caused flames for both people and property.

Samson loved his wife, and the fact that she betrayed him and then was later murdered broke his heart. He began to see women in an entirely new light. First, as objects for his own pleasure. Second, as a way to close his heart and not trust again with a healthy, God-given relationship. He had eyes but was blind to the type of woman God could provide for him.

PRAYER REQUESTS AND PRAYER

Individual Reflection Time - Week 4

Day 1

Let's Relate...

My laser back surgery didn't work like the doctor had promised, so a year later I was faced with *the big surgery*. A cyst had formed on one of my lumbar discs (L3), and it was leaking fluid. The doctors said this was another sign that my back needed surgery and was wearing down. I had been dealing with four herniations (L4-L5-S1) for many years, and the doctor said my back had deteriorated and a fusion was now necessary. By the time I had exhausted all other efforts, I prayed about finding the right surgeon. My appointment was on a Friday afternoon, and, at that point, I required surgery the following Monday.

Because of the rush and needing to leave the doctor quickly to get pre-op bloodwork, EKG, etc. before offices closed, I didn't get the typical time with the doctor to discuss the recovery process and what to expect. The surgery went well, however; waking up from the anesthesia, reality quickly set in as to the road of recovery that stretched out before me.

Let's Explore...

1. **Give an example of a time in your life when you were called to forgive.**

   _____

2. **What helped you through that process?**

   _____

Read 1 John 1:9
Dear Lord, forgiving others is one of the hardest things You call us to do, yet when we don't, we are in direct disobedience to You. You tell us in Your Word that if we don't forgive others, You won't forgive us. We know that when we confess our sins, You are faithful to forgive as You promise in Your Word. Please help me want to forgive and recall anyone that I might be holding unforgiveness against so I can get right with You. Amen.

Day 2

Let's Relate...

Despite having an extremely high energy level, I was forced to lay completely flat or stand for a few minutes at a time. My situation was extremely challenging and frustrating. I am sure my husband felt it almost as much as me, because he experienced my pent-up energy firsthand each evening when he returned from work. David loves to read and wind down after work, and everything he reads is about the Lord. All I wanted to do was talk and interact when he got home, but how does it look when a wife tells her husband to stop reading about the Lord so they can chat? I knew I shouldn't win that one.

The fact was, I couldn't sit for more than one minute at a time those first couple of weeks and then for about three minutes the weeks after that. I was consistently texting the PA to find out if this was normal, and he would continually apologize that we didn't get to discuss my recovery time prior to surgery. I bet he regretted giving me his cell phone number. Little did I know that it would be six weeks before I could sit for any length of time. I thought sitting was highly overrated until this phase of my life. You don't realize how many things are done from a sitting position. I promised I would never complain again about sitting for prolonged periods. I won't go into the white-thigh-high-surgical-hose ordeal for a second time. Now that I was accumulating my own stash of hose, and, with nothing else to do, I began to brainstorm a full marketing campaign and business development opportunity.

Let's Explore...

1. **Did you ever make a covenant or agreement with someone and later change your mind?**

    _____

2. **What made you change your mind, and were there positive or negative consequences?**

    _____

Read James 5:12
Dear Lord, I need to remember not to make empty promises to You, but to let my yes be yes and my no be no, as You say in Your Word in the book of James. Let me be faithful to do what You ask and when I enter into agreement with someone or with You not to waiver, but to stay the course unless You change the course. Give me the strength to remain faithful to Your plan. Amen.

Day 3

Let's Relate...

One night while struggling with boredom, since my life had been reduced to a slow crawl during the recovery period, I remembered that my daughter had given me one of those adult coloring books as a present. They were all the rage for a while, and *they* said coloring would reduce stress and provide relaxing entertainment. I still haven't figured out who *they* are? I asked myself, "Don't I want less stress, relaxation, and something to make the time pass?" I love beautiful pictures and seem to remember enjoying coloring as a child. Earlier, I shared that I have an excessive amount of energy, so imagine all that pent-up energy trying to be channeled into using fine motor skills for an artistic masterpiece. The goal was entertainment, relaxation, experiencing a Zen moment, and—don't forget—a pretty masterpiece.

My first challenge was that I don't like crayons, because the ends become round too fast and make it hard to stay in the lines of the picture. On the flip side, colored pencils need to be sharpened frequently and make annoying scratchy noises. Remember, I am trying this coloring activity to relax. Well, now they have *twist-to-color* crayon sets. All you do is turn them and the color expands! Easy, and they always stay sharp. Talk about innovation—I was so excited to try them and quickly selected my favorite colors.

Let's Explore...

1. **Have you ever done something out of fear of an outcome or because of a threat?**

   _____

2. **Why is the scripture in Romans 12:19 such a challenge for people?**

   _____

Read Deuteronomy 32:35
Dear Lord, I need Your help to remember that it's Yours to avenge when others hurt me. As You say in Deuteronomy, I choose to trust You because You are a just God and will handle situations the way they should be handled. When I take matters into my own hands, I step over Your will and my actions say I'm taking charge. This is not what You would have for me. You always have a plan, and Your way is perfect, and You can see and know things that I may never understand, so I submit to Your will. Amen.

Day 4

Let's Relate...

As I opened the coloring book, I must admit I was perplexed at the strange shapes on each page. The pictures weren't like I remembered as a child. Where were all the trees, castles, princesses, and pretty gardens? Why were there all these tiny, weird geometric shapes shown page after page? I put on my strongest magnifying readers, so I didn't strain my eyes with the small, detailed shapes. I turned on music to allow my creative side to emerge.

About eight minutes in, the picture still looked like a blob, and I realized I still had more than half to color. It felt like a project that would never end. I also tried not to stress by staying in those tiny lines with my new-found crayons. My ADD was off the charts by now, so sitting on the couch coloring and concentrating was a big stretch. Soon my coloring got faster and faster, just so I could finish the picture. I thought I was having fun in the beginning, but now, I wasn't so sure. I felt my pulse racing. "Am I relaxing?" I wondered. "No!" I was on a mission and began to color faster so I could make some headway, but my coloring got messier because of the speed, and now my picture was definitely not pretty.

Let's Explore...

1. **Did you ever nag someone extensively or have you been consistently nagged by someone? Did it work? Why or why not?**

2. **How can we keep our desire for love and pleasure from deceiving us?**

3. **If you are not already married, take some time, and write out the character traits you are looking for in a man. Keep the list in a special place and refer to it when you meet someone new. Re-read it during the first few months of dating to make sure their traits match your list. Don't let infatuation or flattery cause you to ignore the traits you identified as important.**

Read Proverbs 27:15-16 & Colossians 4:6 & 1 Samuel 13:14
Lord, allow me to see quickly when my speech is turning from gentle words into nagging, guilt, or condemnation as that is not how You want me to speak to others. Keep my eyes wide open to see the truth in all situations so I can make wise decisions based on Your plan for my life. (If married) Help me to pray for my husband to be a man after God's own heart as King David was in 1 Samuel. (If single) I pray that you help me identify and find a man after Your own heart. I decide today that I will commit to this prayer and not settle for less in my search. Amen.

Day 5

Let's Relate...

"By golly, I am going to finish this picture tonight," I exclaimed. I realized art is not my thing, and whoever *they* are that said every adult should color to de-stress had no idea what they were talking about. I wanted to meet this *they* and give them a piece of my mind. As I looked down, I saw that I had completed just half of one of the pictures in my book of at least 100 pages of geometric shapes that meant nothing. Additionally, I'd become concerned, because my favorite colors were getting worn down, and I was unable to drive and purchase more, because I still couldn't sit.

I wondered to myself, "What will I do when all I have is the colors I don't like? How will I finish then?" So, I gave up on that page and flipped to another geometric picture with larger shapes, so I would have success at staying in the lines. "Maybe this page will be more fun," I convinced myself. No such luck. Now, I had two unfinished pictures in my book, so I felt like I had not accomplished anything. I was going to have to try something else for entertainment!

Let's Explore...

1. **Write about a time when something happened and you could have reacted badly, but instead you took the time required to respond correctly.**

    _____

2. **What did you do and how did you feel afterwards?**

    _____

Read Isaiah 55:9
Dear Lord, You say in Isaiah 55:9, "As the heavens are higher than the earth, so are My ways higher than your ways and My thoughts than your thoughts." I know that my job is to trust You, obey You, and submit to You. Give me strength to always remember this because many times in the heat of the moment, I forget and need Your gentle reminder. I praise You Lord for Your counsel. Amen.

WEEK 5

THESE ARE MY PEOPLE

DISCUSS: Would anyone like to share about their reflection time this past week?

When we ended last week, we learned that Samson found out his wife had been given to another man. In revenge, Samson caught 300 foxes and tied their tails in pairs with torches. He lit the torches and let the foxes loose in the Philistines' grain fields and vineyards. The Philistines responded in retaliation and burned Samson's wife and her father to death. This leads to another act of revenge by Samson.

Let's Dig In…

Read Judges 15:7-8
Samson said to them, "Since you would do a thing like this, I will surely take revenge on you, and after that I will cease." So he attacked them hip and thigh with a great slaughter; then he went down and dwelt in the cleft of the rock [cave] of Etam.

We now see revenge causing more revenge. Many men were killed because Samson found out his wife was murdered, and he acted in anger. How do you think the Philistines will respond when they find out their people were murdered, on top of Samson destroying their fields and vineyards? Of course, the Philistines are going to head to Judah to locate and get their revenge on Samson. They set up camp to prepare to fight.

Read Judges 15:10
And the men of Judah said, "Why have you come up against us?" So they [Philistines] answered, "We have come up to arrest Samson to do to him as he has done to us."

The Philistines told the men in Judah to surrender Samson, so they could execute their revenge. The problem was Samson wasn't with the men of Judah, because he was hiding in a cave. Three thousand men from Judah went looking for Samson and arrived at the cave in the rock of Etam. This rock must have been like the local coffee shop where everyone hangs out.

Finding Samson, his own people were very angry and lectured him on how he had put their lives in jeopardy. They knew that the Philistines ruled over them and were much more powerful, and Samson had put them in a vulnerable spot through his retaliation and then running away to hide like a coward.

Read Judges 15:11b
…said to Samson, "Do you not know that the Philistines rule over us? What is this that you have done to us?" And he [Samson] said to them, "As they did to me, so I have done to them."

And there is your tit for tat—this type of reaction starts when we're small children and continues into adulthood. I think most of us can agree that revenge will eventually consume our attitudes, thoughts, and sometimes actions. We also see firsthand in this story that each act of retaliation escalates and brings another. How true that still is today. How do we stop the cycle of revenge? God clearly tells us in scripture to leave our hurt, anger, frustration, bitterness, and injustice at His feet, because vengeance should be handled by God alone. The Lord will give us the grace to have mercy and forgiveness on those who bring us harm. This is a process and takes us surrendering ourselves and daily depending on Jesus and His strength. Our job is to pray. Even if we can't get the words out of our mouths to forgive, our job is to pray and ask the Lord, "Help me want to forgive."

DISCUSS: How can unforgiveness halt our walk with the Lord and His plan for us?

Read Judges 15:12-13
But they said to him, "We have come down to arrest you, that we may deliver you into the hand of the Philistines." Then Samson said to them, "Swear to me that you will not kill me yourselves."

Strange thing for Samson to ask of his own people, but, after all, there are three thousand angry men outside this cave. His people agreed and bound him with two new ropes and led him from the rock. Being familiar with Samson's strength and feats, you would think they would have brought something more to restrain him with than two ropes. They seriously underestimated Samson's abilities, but, at this point, he is allowing them to take him to his enemies.

It is interesting to note that this is the first time Israel has formed an army, and it is to capture one of their own people instead of to fight their enemies. If you think about it, many times we do the same. We are more focused on pointing the finger at fellow Christians and the Church instead of our true enemy, which is Satan.

DISCUSS: How do we see this type of divisiveness in our churches and with fellow Christians?

Read Judges 15:14
When he came to Lehi, the Philistines came shouting against him. Then the Spirit of the Lord came mightily upon him; and the ropes that were on his arms became like flax that is burned with fire, and his bonds broke loose from his hands.

We can guess what happens next. Prior to age 40, I wouldn't have understood what flax was. Now that I'm even older, I put it on my oatmeal every morning, so I have a mental image of this scene and what the ropes looked like as they disintegrated to the ground.

Once freed from the ropes, Samson found a fresh jawbone of a donkey. A fresh jawbone is important, because it would be hard, strong, and a perfect weapon, not dry and brittle like old bones become over time. Samson used the jawbone and quickly struck down one thousand men. Amazing for one man to kill a thousand, and it definitely happened because of the power of God being displayed through Samson.

DISCUSS: Did the action above violate his Nazarite vow—why or why not?

Read Judges 15:16
Then Samson said, "With the jawbone of a donkey, Heaps upon heaps, With the jawbone of a donkey I have slain a thousand men."

What do we see here in action? Pride at its finest. The Lord gave Samson strength to battle his enemies, and, instead, he boasted of his own strength and victory. The Philistines had the most advanced weapons, yet they were beaten with a single jawbone of a donkey. Later, King David would defeat Goliath with another simple weapon—a slingshot and a stone—also because the Lord went before David. It is important that we attribute our successes to the Lord and that all glory and honor should go to our Heavenly Father.

God will use whatever is in our hands in our own personal battle to defeat the enemy. No matter how simple or small, with the Spirit of God it becomes a mighty weapon. Samson clearly failed to recognize how the Spirit of the Lord enabled and equipped him to kill his enemies. Like Samson, pride will cause us to take credit for work we've done, when the outcome is always because of God's power and strength.

Judges 15:18
The he [Samson] became very thirsty; so he cried out to the Lord and said, "You have given this great deliverance by the hand of Your servant; and now I shall die of thirst and fall into the hand of the uncircumcised?"

Talk about drama and self-pity. Many times, after a huge effort, or when we are faced with physical needs such as food or rest, our minds are in a vulnerable state. When in a weakened state, it is important not to allow ourselves to get consumed with the thought that God owes us for our efforts or that it is somehow His fault. The "look at me" or "look at what I've done" syndrome is dangerous. It is God's strength that always gives us the victory. After all, He gives us our time, talents, and treasures. We must focus on keeping our attitudes, thoughts, words, and actions on God instead of ourselves. When we keep our eyes focused on Jesus, we see people and situations through Christ's eyes and not our own.

DISCUSS: Can anyone give an example of when the Lord equipped you for a battle or went before you in a difficult situation?

Read Judges 15:19
So God split the hollow place that is in in Lehi, and water came out, and he [Samson] drank; and his spirit returned, and he revived.

God hears our prayers and cares for our physical needs. Scripture tells us that when Samson drank from the place God provided, his strength returned, and he was revived. Sometimes, revenge, pride, or allowing fear to consume us causes panic, and we blame God and cease to trust Him or His provision. This can involve emotional drama or bargaining with God to get Him to bend to our way of thinking, instead of letting Him shape and mold us to His way—which is always higher. If we trust our physical needs to God, He will provide. He is faithful.

Much later…

Twenty years passed, and the Philistines still hated Samson. At this point, he was doing well as a judge, until one day he traveled to the city of Gaza.

Read Judges 16:1
Now Samson went to Gaza, and saw a harlot there, and went in to her.

This account is another example of how Samson's eyes got him into trouble—"He saw a prostitute." As a man set apart for God, it was bad enough for Samson to go to a prostitute, but to do so, he entered enemy territory. This act was Samson's way of taunting his enemies that he was better, smarter, and stronger. This is an example of impulse behavior and following his fleshly desires in the moment. Samson was still haunted by what happened with his wife, and his choices with women continued to spiral downward.

DISCUSS: How can something that haunted you from your past affect your present choices with men?

Read Judges 16:2-3
When the Gazites were told, "Samson has come here!" they surrounded the place and lay in wait for him all night at the gate of the city. They were quiet all night, saying, "In the morning, when it is daylight, we will kill him." And Samson lay low till midnight, took hold of the doors of the gate of the city and the two gateposts, pulled them up, bar and all, put them on his shoulders, and carried them to the top of the hill that faces Hebron.

We should not be surprised that Samson left after having sex with the prostitute and not after spending the entire night. His enemies shouldn't have been surprised, either. After all, these were men, and they should have known better than to think Samson would spend all night with her and wake to cook her breakfast in the morning. Samson sinned, but God did not forget him, nor does He forget us. Samson escaped Gaza with his life, but would he learn his lesson?

He left at midnight, and, when he exited Gaza, he tore out the city guard gate, posts, and bar and carried all of it to the top of the hill at Hebron, about 36 miles away. The Philistine gate at Gaza was at least ten feet high and ten feet wide. The gate would have consisted of two thick doors that could be shut to protect the city with heavy bars, and the side posts were solid and reinforced with metal. The weight of this gate was said to be between five and ten tons. Samson pulled up the guard gate and side posts, which were still attached, as easily as if he'd pulled up a weed.

This was no ordinary human feat of strength. This biblical account is another example of Samson's physical strength, emotional weaknesses, and temptations towards foreign women. This also depicts the frequency at which he wasted his God-given gift of strength in foolish ways.

Enter Delilah...

Just after this account in Gaza, scripture tells us Samson fell in love with another foreign woman, Delilah, who lived in a border town in the Valley of Sorek, which means *Valley of the Choice Vine.* Don't forget Samson was supposed to stay away from grapes, so isn't it interesting that the woman who enraptured him was from a valley meaning choice wine? Scripture says Samson fell in love with Delilah, whose name, ironically enough in Hebrew, means delight, languishing, and temptress. The Hebrew word *delal* means "to weaken."

When we think of Samson, the story with Delilah is the chapter of Judges most of us recognize in the Bible—the tenacious, sexy, and enticing Delilah who enraptured Samson with her beauty and charm. The Philistines had hated Samson for more than 20 years after he burned their fields and killed their people. He had never been the same after the drama with and death of his first wife. Samson should have let go of his pain and trusted God to make things right. Pain, anger, and bitterness consumed him, and now, the Philistines knew his weakness—women. Capitalizing on his weakness, the Philistines hired a woman, Delilah, to trick him and bring him down.

Read Judges 16:4-5
Afterward it happened that he loved a woman in the Valley of Sorek whose name was Delilah. And the lords of the Philistines came to her and said to her, "Entice him, and find out where his great strength lies, and by what means we may overpower him, that we may bind him to afflict him; and every one of us will give you eleven hundred pieces of silver."

There was the bribe—1,100 shekels of silver. Reminds me of Judas being paid to turn Jesus Christ over to the authorities. The Philistines were ruled by five rulers, and each ruled from a different city. Each of these five rulers of the Philistines would pay Delilah, so she was hoping to receive a total of 5,500 shekels. Today, that would be equivalent to almost $90,000. It is no surprise that she wanted to betray Samson when visited by these rich and powerful men. She didn't know Samson well and obviously didn't return his love.

Philistine custom was for men to shave their heads as an outward sign that they were Philistines. The Nazarite custom was to let their hair grow as an outward sign of strength and devotion. The Philistines were not originally from Canaan, and, when they arrived, they learned the Hebrew language but clearly were not Hebrews. The Philistines could speak their language but were still the enemy of the Hebrew people. Delilah could speak Samson's language of love, but the fact is she was still the enemy.

DISCUSS: Our enemy, Satan, uses people who can speak our language, which makes us vulnerable, and we start to believe we are the same when we are really set apart for God. What is another example of how the enemy speaks our language?

When I was a single mom, I met another Christian single mom. We quickly became best friends, but I always knew deep down that her walk was more superficial, and that it was up to me to encourage her to really get to know and live for the Lord. Because we had many things in common due to our situations, we "spoke" the same language. Through it all, I thought I could encourage her in her walk with Christ. I didn't notice that over time, I was being pulled further away in my obedience and walk with the Lord. Sin and separation start subtly, and it's a slow process. This is how sin can seep into our lives, and sometimes it's easy to make excuses when this occurs.

Delilah could speak the Hebrew language, yet she was still the enemy. Delilah also spoke Samson's love language, and the Philistines used his weakness for foreign women. Samson didn't want to lose another woman. Delilah was trying to kill him, and, somewhere deep inside, he had to have known her true intent. Samson thought he could handle the situation. Samson never healed from the past nor surrendered his pain to God and tried to take on the world in his own strength. This will always be our downfall. Samson's purpose was planned by God, but now he brought in his own plan, and this divided his heart, leading to his destruction. God gives us warning signals, so we can flee from destruction, but sometimes we refuse to see the signs.

PRAYER REQUESTS AND PRAYER

Individual Reflection Time - Week 5

Day 1

Let's Relate...

Am I the only one who has trouble staying focused and in the zone during yoga? I started yoga recently to aid during my recovery from major back surgery. *Everyone* kept telling me, "Try yoga—it will make you feel great!" So, I did what any woman would do when given advice by *everyone*, and I invested in a mat, blocks, and new yoga pants. *I'll admit, I already had some yoga pants for days I wanted to eat more chocolate, but I'd never actually practiced yoga!*

My first challenge was breathing. When I breathed as they suggested, I either hyperventilated or got lightheaded, and I know fainting wasn't part of the practice. When I tried to hold my breath longer, I saw myself in the mirror, and I looked purple like Violet, the little girl from the <u>Willy Wonka</u> movie.

Let's Explore...

1. **Have you ever used your influence to sway another person? Explain how.**

    _____

2. **Did you ever wrestle with the Lord?**

    _____

3. **What is another story in the Bible where someone wrestles with God? (Genesis 32:22-31)**

    _____

Read Genesis 32:22-32
Dear Lord, please correct me when I begin to wrestle with You over things and people. Help me to always bring my problems to You first before trying to tackle them on my own, because my way can many times bring undesired outcomes. I know You are faithful to hear my prayers and I trust You and Your counsel. Amen.

Day 2

Let's Relate...

"What's wrong with me?" I wondered. "Why can't I do yoga like the woman in my video?" She made it look effortless! Of course, she was 5'8, skinny as a rail, and about 27 years old. On the other hand, I am in my mid 50's, curvy, and 5'3 on a good day. Remember, I believe in rounding up with height and rounding down with weight for a win-win approach!

Trying to breathe slowly and follow the girl on my computer, I realized how slow the pace was, and I began to think of other things I could be accomplishing. I wondered, "Am I only one whose mind wanders? Am I wasting precious time?" Inadvertently, I found myself breathing faster, hoping it would speed up the yoga practice and I would get done sooner, so I could get more done around the house!

Let's Explore...

1. **Who else in the Bible hid in caves when running from someone or something?**

   _____

2. **Describe a time when you made a choice that carried long-term consequences. Did you ask God to reconsider those consequences? Why or why not?**

   _____

3. **Tell about a time in your life when you realized God's faithfulness in your life.**

   _____

Read 1 Thessalonians 5:24 & Hebrews 6:18-20
Dear Lord, I praise You that You are ALWAYS faithful and You will do what you say. You will never go against your Word. When I doubt Your goodness or faithfulness, remind me to go back to Your Word for the truth. I choose to remind myself of all the times in my past where You were faithful. Thank you for loving me with an everlasting love. I love you too. Amen.

Day 3

Let's Relate...

On the other hand, when I slowed my breathing and poses, I realized I could actually do something else during yoga—like multi-tasking is actually effective! My mind wandered again— "Am I the only one trying to make exercise also productive?" Then rationality hit, and I said to myself, "Doesn't this defeat the reason for doing yoga in the first place?" I suppose it matters why you take up yoga. After all, I was doing it to strengthen my core and stretch my back, not necessarily for relaxation and focus. As I write this, I realize that maybe I should be doing it for relaxation and focus!

Posing in the downward dog position, I learned to balance on my left hand and answer email messages with my right hand, if I used voice dictation. I could also throw a tennis ball for my puppy, because, for some reason, she likes to play while I am upside down. When I played a game of fetch, I actually got a little bit of a stretch in between ball throws, before she jumped up and grabbed my hair again.

Let's Explore...

1. **What is another Biblical account of another woman who acted deceitfully? (Read Genesis 27:5-17)**

   _____

2. **What do you think motivated the wife/mother in the scripture above to be deceptive?**

   _____

Read 1 Peter 3:10
Dear Lord, thank you that You so clearly define in Your Word things that will keep me from harm and keep me on paths of righteousness. I want to use my time and talents for good and not in selfish or manipulative ways. Please show me when I unconsciously or consciously act in ways that are not honoring to You and others. Amen.

Day 4

Let's Relate…

Psalm 46:10 says, "Be still, and know that I am God." What an amazing verse. Yet being a half-century in age, *(pause—I took a break for some chocolate because this fact just hit me)*, I realized *being still and trusting God* was something I still need to master. Why can't I just learn to relax and trust my Creator who can truly handle my issues and mishaps? Why can't I learn to be STILL, to meditate on God's goodness, to read His Word, to relax in stillness, and worry less? Why can't I eliminate the *what if* game from my vocabulary? Do I really need to play out all the scenarios in my head, so I can resolve each one of them, instead of relying on my Heavenly Father in ALL things?

Instead of being still, why do I need to be doing something all the time: listening to music, watching a movie, shopping, running errands, meeting up with friends, exercising? Did God write this verse just for me?

Let's Explore…

1. **How does it affect our communication with Christ when we sin? Do you still easily go to Him afterwards?**

   _____

2. **Where is an account in the Bible where another man of God confessed his sins? (Read 2 Samuel 12:13)**

   _____

3. **Even though God forgave the him, what were the lasting consequences from his sin?**

   _____

Read Luke 15:7 & Psalm 139:23-24
Dear Lord, Thank you for Your great mercy and love for me. You are faithful to forgive and all of heaven rejoices when I come to You in repentance. I know when I sin, it becomes easier to hide from You out of guilt and remorse. I praise You that I don't have to do that. Search my heart Lord and keep it pure. I love you Jesus. Amen.

Day 5

Let's Relate...

As I speak with more and more women, they also seem to struggle with the concept of being still, which creates a cycle of worry and anxiety. Is it a sign of our times and busy multimedia society, which causes us to feel the need to be in constant control? One would have to say, "No," because the Bible was written long ago, and because God created us and knows our human nature is not to BE Still and to struggle to fully trust Him.

Imagine how we might be able to relax and hear Christ if only we could wrap our heads around this simple concept. We would experience less stress, anxiety, depression, and fewer identity crises. We would probably eat less ice cream and chocolate during times of difficulty as well! Comprehension of this simple yet profound Bible verse would allow us to experience God's peace, relaxation, rejuvenation, and fulfillment. Who wouldn't want all these wonderful gifts from our Heavenly Father?

Let's Explore...

1. **Why do you think Samson tore up the gates as he left the city in the middle of the night?**

   _____

2. **This account shows Samson acting on temptation without thinking it through. Does this make you think of a situation in your own life where you did the same? If so, how did you feel in the days following the event?**

   _____

Read Romans 12:19 & Hebrews 10:30
Dear Lord, anger can take root quickly and I can act without thinking. Please guide me in my responses and help me to always remember to bring them to You first to avoid calamity. You tell us in both Romans and Hebrews that vengeance belongs to You. When I begin to take matters into my own hands, please quickly remind me the truth and to surrender to You. You are a just God, and I trust You. When I am weak, You are strong. Amen.

WEEK 6

PLEADING – WILL IT REALLY WORK?

DISCUSS: Does anyone want to share something they learned during their reflection time this past week?

Let's Dig In...

Read Judges 16:6
So Delilah said to Samson, "Please tell me where your great strength lies, and with what you may be bound to afflict you." (Note: this is the first time she asks)

Remember that Samson was enraptured by her beauty, but he was still skeptical of her character. He immediately gave her a false answer.

Read Judges 16:7
And Samson said to her, "If they bind me with seven fresh thongs not yet dried, then I shall become weak, and be like any other man."

Now I know you're wondering what a thong is, and I wish I could tell you what it meant back then. My mother would tell you it's what I refer to as a flip-flop. Mom would always tell me to put on my thongs before leaving the house. Victoria's Secret would give you another definition. As I've gotten older, we've had several debates over this term especially when we are in public. I could look up the historical meaning, but that would take all the fun out of this paragraph.

Read Judges 16:8
Then the rulers of the Philistines brought her seven fresh bowstrings that had not been dried, and she tied him with them.

Samson must have been a heavy sleeper to not feel himself being tied up. Think about Delilah's boldness to try to tie up a man as powerful as Samson.

Read Judges 16:9-10
Now men were lying in wait, staying with her in the room. And she said to him, "The Philistines are upon you, Samson!" But he broke the bowstrings as a strand of yarn breaks when it touches fire. So the secret of his strength was not known. Then Delilah said to Samson, "Look you have mocked me and told me lies. Now please tell me what you may be bound with." (Note: this is the second time she asks)

At this point, Delilah had asked him twice how he maintained his incredible strength. You must admit she was bold to try this on more than one occasion. Talk about turning the table on blame—sometimes women can be masters at this. Samson, on the other hand, must have been a little slow on the uptake. He didn't seem to notice or care. Samson could kill beasts and 1,000 men but not manage his lust for a woman and see Delilah for who she clearly was, even after one attempt to trick him. Delilah didn't care about Samson and was obsessed by the financial bribe.

DISCUSS: It helps to decide what kind of a person you will love long before you meet them. Why is this important before we begin the infatuation phase?

Infatuation and temptation can blind us to traits or behaviors that are warning signals. Before dating, determine whether a person's character and faith in God are as desirable as their physical appearance. This way you won't miss red flags during those euphoric first few months and even first year. Remember that most of the time you spend with your spouse over the years will be in conversation and companionship—not focused as heavily on their physical attributes.

Read Judges 16:11
So he said to her, "If they bind me securely with new ropes that have never been used, then I shall become weak and be like any other man."

Why didn't Samson tell her the truth at this point? Was he being true to his vow? Maybe he was enjoying the game of back and forth but still didn't trust her. Or maybe, he was just plain being stubborn.

Read Judges 16:12-13a
Therefore Delilah took new ropes and bound him with them, and said to him, "The Philistines are upon you, Samson!" And men were lying in wait, staying in the room. But he broke them off his arms like thread. Delilah said to Samson, "Until now, you have mocked me and told me lies. Tell me what you may be bound with." (Note: this is the third time she asks)

Delilah didn't acknowledge her own lies, manipulation, and deception. Samson didn't seem to notice. He offers another explanation—that if she wove his seven braids of hair on his head into the fabric on the loom and tightened it with the pin, he would then become as weak as any other man.

I would have loved to have been inside Samson's head. What must he be thinking about the woman he chose to be with—seriously? Not surprisingly, while he was sleeping, she wove the seven braids of his head into the fabric of the loom and tightened it with the pin. He must have taken a sleeping pill to not wake during this attempt. Again, she told him the Philistines were there to capture him. He awoke from his sleep and pulled the pin and the loom with the fabric, releasing his hair and freeing himself.

Read Judges 16:15-16
Then she said to him, "How can you say, 'I love you' when your heart is not with me? You have mocked me these three times and have not told me where your great strength lies." And it came to pass, when she pestered him daily with her words and pressed him, so that his soul was vexed to death.

Delilah should have been an actress. She constantly hounded Samson, and it became so exhausting that he said he wanted to die, ironically foreshadowing the future. Don't forget that his former wife did the same thing. Why would Samson continue to fall into this trap? Could he have been blind to her tricks because of her beauty and his love?

Let's think about the lesson here. How many of us have ever continuously nagged a man? I'll admit it, I have. And I'll admit I can be very good at it. Has someone ever nagged or pressured you? Delilah was cold and calculating because of her motive to get rich. She not only gave of herself intimately to get a financial reward, but she also pretended to love him. When a man is nagged to the point of exhaustion, he will typically respond in one of three ways: withdraw, give in, or give up.

DISCUSS: Why do men respond the way they do when consistently nagged by a woman?

How could Samson be so foolish—three times he allowed Delilah to trick him. We think he is foolish, because it is easy to spot what's happening, since we are reading it in the Bible, but how many times do we allow ourselves to be deceived by flattery and give in to temptation or false beliefs? It is important to spend time with God daily and ask Him for wisdom to help us distinguish between deception and truth.

Delilah always attacked when Samson fell asleep. On every occasion, she waited, because he was vulnerable when he was asleep. Samson laid his head in her lap, because he was tired, and it looked like a safe place. Sometimes when we lay our head down, we mistake it for a safe place. Our enemy knows this, and it is amazing how tempting a lap will appear when we are weary. The enemy always attacks when we're tired and our defenses are down, when we aren't focused on God, not praying, or spending time in His Word. Satan knows when we are tired and weary and comes in for the kill. We can't fight the good fight when we are worn down, haven't eaten, haven't slept, or aren't wearing our spiritual battle equipment. We will lose every time.

Re-Read Judges 16:15a
Then she said to him, "How can you say you, 'I love you' when your heart is not with me?"

When Delilah makes this statement, she goes for Samson's heart. This becomes about a heart move—not a haircut. Samson was foolish to get involved with another Philistine woman. He should have known from the beginning that she had her own agenda. The power of "love" was so strong over Samson that he would not stop spending time with Delilah, so he didn't get the time he needed with God to think clearly. He should have run the other direction.

DISCUSS: How carefully do you guard your feelings and your passions? How many people bring calamity into their lives and the lives of their loved ones by not guarding their feelings? What is the best way to protect ourselves from this trap?

The best marriage, friendship, or relationship should bring each person closer to God, not drive one or the other person away. We see clearly how spending time with the wrong kind of person can begin to lead someone away from the Lord.

It is interesting to compare Samson's first wife and Delilah: both women were Philistines, and the Philistine leaders asked both women to trap Samson. At first, Samson would not let either woman trap him. But, in the end, Samson gave in to both. Samson did not marry Delilah, but it's her name, not that of his nameless wife, that we remember when we think of Samson.

Every time Samson is tied up, he is sleeping, so one can wonder if he is vulnerable because he is tired. Through bleary eyes, Delilah's words somehow sounded reasonable, even though the Bible describes his soul as being vexed to death.

Read Judges: 16:17
…that he told her all his heart, and said to her, "No razor has ever come upon my head for I have been a Nazarite to God from my mother's womb. If I am shaven, then my strength will leave me, and I shall become weak, and be like any other man."

Samson obviously remembered his vow to God but must have wanted to stop the games and nagging and come clean. When Delilah realized this time that he was telling the truth, she again sent word to the rulers of the Philistines who returned with the bribe money and hid in the room to wait.

Samson took his covenant with God and traded it for stolen moments with Delilah. He lost his heart before he lost his hair. At the very moment his covenant was given away, his strength left him, because God left him. Now his enemies easily captured him.

Read Judges 16:19-20
Then she lulled him to sleep on her knees, and called for a man and had him shave off the seven locks of his head. Then she began to torment him, and his strength left him. And she said, "The Philistines are upon you, Samson!" So he awoke from his sleep, and said, "I will go out as before, at other times, and shake myself free!" But he did not know that the Lord had departed from him.

God had been very patient with him for a long time. But when Samson gave himself over to the power of sin and told Delilah his secret, the Lord's Spirit left him. There was no power in his long hair, as it was just an example of his trust in and allegiance to God. So, when Samson's vow to God was sacrificed for lust, he also lost his strength. I suppose Samson thought God's grace and mercy would continue to cover him always, but he'd tested God one too many times.

DISCUSS: Even when we love and serve the Lord, how should we watch for danger when we become tired or weary?

How many times have we succumbed to flattery and deceit because of who was giving it? Maybe he was someone powerful, rich, handsome, popular, or even someone we never thought would notice us. Then, we allowed ourselves to succumb to the temptation to be noticed or accepted during that one powerful moment we thought would last forever. But it only lasts for a short time and carries huge repercussions. We need to continually ask God to help us be wise and recognize the difference between a truth and a lie and not let our emotions dictate our actions.

Read Judges 16:21
Then the Philistines took him and put out his eyes and brought him down to Gaza. They bound him with bronze fetters, and he became a grinder in the prison.

The Philistines immediately seized him, bound him with bronze shackles, gouged out his eyes, and transported him to Gaza to grind grain in the local prison. Gaza was the same city he had entered to taunt his enemies and sleep with a prostitute. Now, he was back again as a slave. Samson, the mighty warrior, became Samson, the slave. His enemies could have easily killed him but preferred to humiliate him instead.

Long before his eyes were poked out, Samson was blinded by sin and desire. He tested God one too many times and thought nothing would happen when he sinned. Our sin always brings consequences, whether physical, mental, or spiritual. Sin always blinds us and hold us captive, like Samson was in prison. When blinded by sin, we can't experience the joy or strength of the Lord, and we are separated from him until we repent. It is interesting that both the strongest man in the Bible, Samson, and the wisest man in the Bible, Solomon, were both taken down by their temptations and lust of women.

DISCUSS: Embezzlers usually start out stealing a few pencils or a small amount of money. Not many people think, "I will start stealing thousands or millions from my company." The same with adultery; it starts with a sly smile or simple flirtation to test the waters. What's your view on "big" sins versus "small" sins? What do you think God's view is?

In prison, Samson had lots of time to wonder if Delilah's beauty was worth spending the rest of his life as a blind slave. The Philistines had gouged out the very parts of his body that got him into this predicament, taking away his freedom and reducing him to being a captured slave and town mockery. Samson ground grain in a wheel going around and around in a circle. There are times in our lives when we are wondering why life feels like a grind and why we are going in circles, when it is the result of our sin. A little compromise here and there with sin always leads to a bigger issue later.

DISCUSS: What happens when we take the "God's love" part of the Bible and assume that obedience doesn't matter or that the Bible doesn't really mean what it says—at least for modern times?

Read Judges 16:22
However, the hair of his head began to grow again after it had been shaven.

Samson's hair grew back, but his eyesight never returned. Certain things are lost forever because of sin.

Read Galatians 6:7-9
Do not be deceived: God is not mocked; for whatever a man sows, that he will also reap. For he who sows to his flesh, will of the flesh reap corruption, but he who sows to the Spirit will of the Spirit reap everlasting life. And let us not grow weary while doing good, for in due season we shall reap [harvest] if we do not lose heart.

DISCUSS: Even though God is always faithful to forgive when we repent, does the consequence always get removed? How does the verse in Galatians address trusting God even when we can't see the harvest (outcome)?

Read Judges 16:23 & 25-26
Now the lords of the Philistines gathered together to offer a great sacrifice to Dagon their god, and to rejoice. And they said: "Our god has delivered into our hands Samson our enemy!" So it happened, when their hearts were merry, that they said, "Call for Samson that he may perform for us." So they called for Samson from the prison, and he performed for them. And they stationed him between the pillars. Then Samson said to the lad who held him by the hand, "Let me feel the pillars which support the temple, so that I can lean on them."

Samson was taken to Gaza, which is the same place where he'd earlier showed his superior strength when he uprooted the city gates. Dagon, a grain and fertility god, was the chief god of the Philistines, and they built many temples for worship and human sacrifice. When the scripture says "perform" in this context, it means to entertain through ridicule. In that day, the temples were the places where torture and prisoner humiliation took place as a form of entertainment for the crowds. They would gather and sit on the flat temple roof to see the entertainment in the courtyard below.

Remember that Samson was now blind, with his hands and feet shackled by chains. God can only be good, and it's the enemy who comes to steal, kill, and destroy (John 10:10). God didn't altogether abandon Samson, but he did let Samson's pride and decision to go his own route bring with it natural consequences, leading him into this devastating situation. God gives each of us free will and choice. God loves us, and His heart aches for us when we make choices that carry painful consequences—some of them significant and permanent. Samson didn't think his choice would lead to his slavery, but it was the consequence for his choice to experience those fleeting moments of satisfaction with Delilah and to disobey his Nazarite vow.

Back on the roof, the Philistines were having a huge party to celebrate Samson's capture, because he had been a thorn in their side for quite some time. They were worshiping their god Dagon and chastising Samson for entertainment, bragging while drinking and partying, thus explaining their high spirits. Scripture says the temple was crowded with men and women, which included all the rulers of the Philistines—on the roof alone there were about 3,000 people.

Now, let's go back to the last verse in Judges chapter 16, just before it describes this party on the roof, to re-read very important words.

Read Judges 16:22
However, the hair of his head began to grow again after it had been shaven.

We all know what this means. Samson's hair is returning, and with that comes his strength, but not because of his hair. Samson humbled himself and realized he was forging his own path and had not let God lead. He had tried doing it his way, and, when he realized this, he repented and asked God to give him his strength just once more. God is always listening and always working. Our job is to believe, trust, repent, and obey.

PRAYER REQUESTS AND PRAYER

INDIVIDUAL REFLECTION TIME - WEEK 6

Day 1

Let's Relate...

As I approached another birthday, I used this as the excuse to talk my hubby into getting me a puppy! Sadly, I'd had to put my last dog down a few years ago and hadn't been able to bring myself to get another pet, as it was painful to say goodbye. I'd always loved pets and found them a great source of comfort, companionship, and laughter—especially puppies! What I didn't remember was how much work puppies were, since I had my previous dog for so many years.

Initially my husband said no, but I used all available female influence and reminded him that a puppy would be a welcome distraction from my day-to-day struggle of back pain. To seal the deal, I batted my eyes and reminded him of my approaching 50th birthday, and he finally conceded! *Nothing like good ol' fashioned female persuasion mixed with guilt and sympathy!* The search for the perfect dog began, and after much research we decided upon a malti-poo.

Let's Explore...

1. **Think back to the last time you went through a huge undertaking. Were you exhausted or rejuvenated?**

   _____

2. **Did you do anything differently the next time you had a similar job or task?**

   _____

3. **Read 1 Kings chapters 18-19 and list below another time when someone let fear consume them after a huge victory and needed God's provision for food and revival.**

   _____

Diana S. Perez

Read 2 Timothy 1:7

Dear Lord, You will give me the victory if I just trust and rely on You. When I turn from You and try to do things in my own strength, I can get tired and easily defeated. Just like the victory You gave Elijah, he quickly forgot and let fear overtake him and lost his confidence in You. Help me to mediate on the verse in 2 Timothy and remember that You never give us a spirit of fear. I love you Lord. Amen.

Day 2

Let's Relate...

I wanted a female dog this time, because my former dog was male, and he seemed to have the need to *mark* everything. *No clue what that was all about!* If you pay attention in the work environment, you may see this same behavior with males—but that is a story for another time. We picked up our puppy, who was 10 weeks old, and named her "Lucy," as I have always loved that name. It seemed to match her fun, cute personality. She weighed about four pounds and was perfect, because we lived in a small townhouse. Lucy quickly grew and became accustomed to our home and receiving so much unmerited attention and love!

One day, while she stood on my lap while we were on the couch, I started to rub her tummy. You're probably wondering why I had to rub her tummy while she stood—well, Lucy didn't seem to be able to relax and lay on her back. She didn't yet trust me. Dogs laying on their backs is not a natural position and takes quite a bit of trust of their situation. Speaking gently to her as if she could understand, I said, "Lucy—I know you love when I rub your tummy. Why don't you lay back and just relax? This will feel so good if you would just lay down. I promise you will enjoy it." She tried to lay back, as she loved me rubbing her belly, but would quickly pop back up to a standing position almost immediately.

Let's Explore...

1. **Share a time when you accomplished a huge task or had something big to overcome.**

    _____

2. **What was the outcome, and did you receive a reward? How did you feel afterward?**

    _____

Read Isaiah 54:10
Dear Lord, I have so many things to do and sometimes I get overwhelmed. Please help me remember that You are in charge, and You go before me. When I get tired, help me to come to You for rejuvenation so I don't get weary in the battle and give up or give in. I know You love me, and Your covenant of peace will not be removed as You promise in Isaiah. Amen.

Day 3

Let's Relate…

Then it hit me, and I realized it is the same thing when God tries to lavish His love on me. Do I relax and just rest in His love and blessings, or do I force my way back up and get too busy to enjoy just being loved? Do I accept His love without question, or do I fight against it, since unmerited love isn't easy to accept? Do I try to *be good or do good* to earn His love, when He just wants me to rest and enjoy His presence?

One of my favorite Psalms is 46:5: "God is with her. She WILL not fall." The world can be a challenging place filled with difficulties and sorrow, until we have the opportunity to spend eternity in a perfect place—Heaven. What God is saying in this scripture is that, ultimately, He has won the battle, and, because we are secure in Him, we will also win the battle.

Let's Explore…

1. **What do you think about what Delilah did given the period of that day?**

   _____

2. **Have you ever let others entice you with their looks, strength, money, or security? Why is security typically important to most women?**

   _____

Read Psalm 40:2 & Proverbs 31
Dear Lord, don't let me ever compromise my values for money, popularity, other people, or status. I want to be a virtuous woman like the woman in Proverbs 31, but I need Your help to stay true to Your will and to walk in Your ways. If I stay focused on You, then I succeed, but when I try to do things in my own flesh, I get tired and fail. You promise to set my feet upon a rock and I cling to Your promises. Amen.

Day 4

Let's Relate...

Winning the battle doesn't mean life will be without issues. People make the mistake of thinking that life is supposed to be easy, because God created the world, but they forget about the fall in the garden of Eden. Adam and Eve willingly made the choice to sin (they couldn't just rest and enjoy the perfection of how it should have been—just enjoy God's blessings like I was trying to get Lucy to do). Once sin entered the world, it brought in sorrow, anguish, imperfection, and disease.

What God promises us in this world is not a picture-perfect time on earth—what He promises us is found in several places in the Bible, one of which is in Deuteronomy 31:8: "The Lord himself goes before you and will be with you; He will never leave you nor forsake you. Do not be afraid; do not be discouraged."

Let's Explore...

1. **Explain how you may have let your beauty, charm, talents, or intelligence be used in ways God didn't intend.**

   _____

2. **Where is the best place to get the truth regarding where we can obtain our confidence?**

   _____

Read Ephesians 3:12 & Hebrews 4:16
Dear Lord, Help me always remember to boldly come to You for my confidence as this definition is the truth and Your love for me is unparallel. May I be reminded often of the wonderful verse and promise in Deuteronomy above. Because of Your love, I never need to do things that are beneath me and what Your will is for my life. I praise You alone Abba Daddy. Amen.

Day 5

Let's Relate…

God promises to always love us, to never leave us, and to walk with us in the good times and bad. To believe otherwise is contradictory to the definition of faith, which is believing in something you can't see or touch. We trust the diagnosis from a doctor we barely know and the prescription he writes when we can't even read it. What about if the pharmacy fills the wrong prescription? Why can we trust the doctor easier than we trust our Creator of the universe?

Is this why Lucy has trouble knowing that I only want to provide her comfort when I rub on her tummy—trouble relaxing and enjoying the feeling that I know she will like? If she would only lay back, she would experience a lavishing of love—what if we could do the same?

Let's Explore…

1. **Is there a choice you have made that has carried lasting consequences?**

   _____

2. **Write your thoughts when you read the scripture in Judges 16:22.**

   _____

Read Jonah 2:1-2 & Re-read Psalms 40:2
Dear Lord, Your Word is filled with so many promises for others who have been given second, third, and even fourth chances. You are always faithful to forgive, and I know that even if my feet slip in the clay, You will plant them once again on Your rock. Thank you for Your mercy, care, and compassion. I adore you Lord. Amen.

WEEK 7

DON'T FORGET ME, LORD

DISCUSS: Does anyone want to share anything from what we have studied so far in the Samson series?

Samson had tested God one time too many times, just like we may do when we don't experience an immediate consequence to sinning. As a Nazarite, he shouldn't have touched grapes, yet he did, and God didn't take his strength to defeat a lion away. He shouldn't have touched a dead body, yet he did, and God didn't take his strength to kill 1,000 men away.

In his mind, he probably figured that nothing would happen if he told the secret about his hair to Delilah. He tested God. We do the same when we rationalize the Bible is a multiple-choice option list, especially when we have gotten away with it in the past without consequences. Obedience to God doesn't work this way. After all this time, Samson was probably shocked when he woke and found that his strength was actually gone.

Let's Dig In…

Read Judges 16:28
Then Samson called to the Lord saying, "O Lord God, remember me, I pray! Strengthen me, I pray, just this once, O God, that I may with one blow take vengeance on the Philistines for my two eyes."

Samson was humbled in prison and realized his mistake in breaking his covenant with the Lord on multiple occasions. He also realized his love was misplaced with Delilah, and that he chose her over his obedience to the Lord. He began his prayer with first acknowledging our Great Almighty by saying, **"O Sovereign Lord."** He then humbly asked the Lord to acknowledge him as His beloved child. Samson wanted revenge for more than the loss of his two eyes and was also seeking redemption for the loss of his freedom and dignity. Samson then stated his case and explained how they'd captured and tortured him and were trying to amuse themselves at his expense, all to benefit their foreign god. Samson knew the one true God.

DISCUSS: Have you ever felt like God forgot you?

Samson admitted that even though he disobeyed God, he had not forgotten Him or His great power, and he didn't think God had forgotten him. We need to consistently search our hearts and ask the Lord if there is anything we need to reconcile, deal with, or confess. Samson prayed once more to a merciful God to reconsider and renew his strength so that he may show his enemies what someone can do through God's power and strength.

There is a verse in Matthew 18:9 that says, ***And if your eye causes you to sin, pluck it out and cast it from you.***

DISCUSS: What do you think this verse means?

Samson had both his eyes plucked out, because his eyes had gotten him into this predicament in the first place. Remember Samson's first words to his parents, "Get her for me for she pleases me"—he admired her physical beauty with his eyes. He was punished accordingly for letting his flesh overrule God's plan for his life.

DISCUSS: How many of us have ever missed the boat and felt the Lord speaking to us but we didn't respond?

I have. I was traveling for work, and, as I was leaving my hotel room late to meet my client, I looked over and saw the housekeeper coming out of another room. The Lord impressed upon my heart to give her the cash that was in my wallet and tell her, "God loves you." Of course, I first asked, "Is that you, God? She is going to think I'm strange, I only have a small amount of money, and I'm already late. How about if I find her later and give her the money and your message then?"

I was too busy at the time to follow through on what God had asked me to do. I thought He would understand how busy I was, because I was a single mom and working long hours. Later, realizing my mistake and feeling regret, I tried to make up for it the next day, but it was too late. I never saw her again. God's timing is perfect, and He always has a plan. She must have needed to feel His love in a tangible way that day, and I missed the boat. I have never forgotten that lesson, albeit through a simple task that the Lord gave me. God gives second chances (and third, and fourth…) when we repent and ask for His help.

God gave me another similar opportunity about several years later, but this time He upped the ante and asked me to give quite a bit more than He did the first time. This time, I responded with, "I see this as an opportunity to give and share Your love, Lord. I won't make the same mistake again, so I'll gladly hit the ATM across the lobby and became the hands and feet of Christ." I gave the stranger the message: "God wants you to have this and wants me to tell you how much He loves you," I barely got my message out through teared eyes as she also responded in tears. Afterwards, I prayed, "Thanks for letting me do Your work today, Lord—it is amazing to be part of Your plan and see it play out."

DISCUSS: Anyone want to share about a second or third chance the Lord gave them?

Read Judges 16:29-30a
And Samson took hold of the two middle pillars which supported the temple, and he braced himself against them, one on his right and the other on his left. Then Samson said, "Let me die with the Philistines!"

Samson offered his life to God rather than make demands from God. Accountability is closely associated with humility. Humility is the root from the word humiliation, which is what happened to Samson when he was reduced to being a prisoner and became entertainment for his enemies. Samson's prayer was humble, and he became vulnerable. The pride and mockery he once displayed were gone.

Don't wait until it is believed to be too late to use your talents and follow God's will for your life. Life is precious, and I think those of us who are older know that time passes much quicker than we realized when we were young.

Samson had amazing gifts from the Lord and could have used them to powerfully move in the lives of others. Not many people start life with credentials like his. Samson was born because of God's plan for Manoah and his wife. He was specifically created and chosen to do a great work for the Lord and begin the deliverance of Israel from the hands of the Philistines. However, Samson wasted his enormous gift of strength on jokes, revenge, and getting out of difficult situations that he himself had orchestrated. He eventually gave up his gift from God to satisfy his infatuation with an enticing and deceitful woman.

DISCUSS: Do we ever wonder why God puts us in a difficult situation and later realize it was us who put ourselves there?

Read Judges 16:30b
And he pushed with all his might, and the temple fell on the lords and all the people who were in it. So the dead that he killed at his death were more than he had killed in his life.

In the end and in his distress, Samson prayed to God, who still answered his prayer despite Samson's disobedience. God heard Samson's prayer of confession and repentance and used him in this one final act to destroy the pagan temple and the idolatrous worshipers contained within and around its walls.

Samson killed more people when he died than all the time he'd lived. His greatest moment wasn't in the years of deterring the Philistines but at the moment of his death. God loved Samson just as He loves each of us, even when we stray and are disobedient.

When we continue to choose to sin or make bad choices in life, one of the outcomes is that it keeps us from wanting to pray because of guilt and shame. How many of us have experienced that? It makes us not want to go to God and ask for answers to prayers, healing, or blessings, and it makes it hard to praise and worship Him, because we feel guilty about our actions. Facing a perfect and glorious God is extremely difficult in moments like these. It's a little like trying to look your parent or spouse in the eye when they're asking you a question, and you know you're not telling the truth.

Read Psalms 103:8-12
The Lord is merciful and gracious, Slow to anger, and abounding in mercy. He will not always strive with us, Nor will He keep His anger forever. He has not dealt with us according to our sins, Nor punished us according to our iniquities. For as the heavens are high above the earth, So great is His mercy toward those who fear him; As far as the east is from the west, So far He has removed our transgressions from us.

DISCUSS: Is perfection a pre-requisite for prayer to our Heavenly Father?

This is the very place Satan wants to keep us—feeling like we can't go to God, because we've made a mistake. No matter how long we have stayed away from the Lord—one day, one week, one month, one year, or more—the Lord is patiently waiting for us to confess and come back into His loving arms. As the scripture so eloquently states in the verse in Psalms above, He has separated our sins as far as from the east to the west. Think about the distance from New York to California. It is us who sometimes think we have to cling to our sins, our past, or our way of life.

Christ wants to restore the relationship, and He longs to forgive us, no matter how big the mistake. This doesn't mean there won't be consequences for our actions. If we speed when driving, we could get a ticket. If we cheat at our job, we could get fired. If someone has sex outside of the confines of marriage, they could get a disease. The good news is that praying to God, asking, and receiving His forgiveness is our only means of restoration of His grace, mercy, and peace in our lives. We then need to get back up, dust ourselves off, and continue to run the race He has for our lives. God's plan for us is always better than our own plan.

In conclusion, Samson led and was a judge in Israel for twenty years in the days of the Philistines. His judgeship consisted of single-handed victories over the Philistines, which disrupted their domination over Israel. Samson did not, however, liberate Israel from the Philistine oppression. That was not God's plan for his life. Samson was to begin the job. Sometimes in life we want the victory or the final result, but God may want us to play a different role. The important thing is that we are obedient to the task to which God has called us, so we don't miss being part of His incredible plan. Now don't misunderstand: God will always accomplish His plan, but we may miss out on being part of it if we're not willing or obedient (Isaiah 1:19).

Although Samson often used poor judgment on many occasions, he accomplished quite a bit when he determined he would be set apart for God. In this way, Samson was like the nation of Israel. As long as Israel remained focused on God, the nation thrived; however, when they ignored God, they fell back into sin and tough consequences.

Read Revelation 3:16 "So then, because you are lukewarm, and neither hot nor cold—I will vomit you out of My mouth."

Simply put, Samson had one foot in (the things of God) and one foot out, which is an easy way to explain the scripture in the book of Revelation. How many of us can blame him? How many of us live one way on Saturday night and another on Sunday morning? Our job is to daily die to our sins, ask for forgiveness, and then walk in the grace and mercy which He gives. God is always faithful to forgive when we sin, so it is important that we quickly repent and get right with our Heavenly Father, so we can continue in the journey He has for us. The choice is ours.

DISCUSS: Share examples of having one foot in and one foot out in today's times.

Amazing abilities or talents in one area of life do not make up for weaknesses in other areas. I don't want to be remembered for what might have been. Sometimes, I imagine standing before Christ trying to explain or giving excuses for my choices. Whatever I say, it sounds lame, as I begin to hear myself state my explanation out loud to the Lord.

DISCUSS: What does the verse Lamentations 3:22-23 tell us about God's grace? What hope does this give us?

Do you think Samson accomplished his plan? We think Samson wasted his life and the role God had for him, because he ended up grinding grain in prison, and then he tragically died instead of helping his people. He could've helped extinguish the Philistines and led his people in worshiping God. Samson's story teaches us that it's never too late to start over. Remember that Samson still accomplished the purpose announced by the angel before he was born. In his last moments, Samson began to rescue Israel from the Philistines.

In the end, Samson recognized his dependence on God. When he died, God turned his failure and defeats into a victory. Samson is listed in Hebrews chapter 11 as a faithful follower of the Lord and as one of the few men inducted into God's *Hall of Faith*. So even though Samson made many bad choices, God still saw something in Samson that made him worthy. The Apostle Peter got it right in the end as well. He denied Christ several times, but, in the end, he loved and served the Lord faithfully. Peter was righteous. Samson was righteous. We, too, are righteous, because God says we are (2 Corinthians 5:21), and we must begin to see ourselves through God's eyes.

P R A Y E R   R E Q U E S T S   A N D   P R A Y E R

Describe what most impacted you about Samson's life story and any areas in your own life you may change or adjust going forward from this Bible study.

In Closing

There is so much revelation in God's Word, and we simply touched on a few points in our seven weeks together. Read and decree out loud the Apostle Paul's prayers for the church in Ephesians 1:16-23; 3:14-20, and Colossians 1:9-11 regarding God's promises for receiving wisdom and revelation. Make these prayers your own. Pray and ask God to expand your mind to give you a deeper revelation and show you specifically how to apply His Word to your life and daily walk with Him.

Dear Lord,

You have gifted me in many ways, and You have a plan for my life, as Your Word states in Jeremiah 29:11. Your Word says a virtuous woman is more valuable than rubies. I know that while I am a sinner, You are always faithful to forgive as it is written in 1 John 1:9. I accept Your forgiveness and know that You have washed me clean, and now I ask for Your help to forgive myself. As I strive to study Your Word, spend time in prayer, and take a step closer to You each day, I know that You will bless me, keep me, and uphold me with Your righteous right hand. Amen.

I hope this study has blessed you.

Prayer of Salvation:
Are you saved? If not, say this prayer out loud to receive Christ:

I believe in my heart that Jesus is the Son of God. I believe Jesus died for my sins and was raised from the dead so I can be in right-standing with God. I am calling upon the name of Jesus, so I know, Father that You saved me now. Amen.

Printed in the United States
by Baker & Taylor Publisher Services